# Drink!

Copyright © Bruce Anderson (text) 2020
Copyright © Lachy Campbell (illustrations) 2020

First published in the UK in 2020 by
Quiller, an imprint of Quiller Publishing Ltd

British Library Cataloguing-in-Publication Data
A catalogue record for this book is available from
the British Library

ISBN 978-1-84689-330-8

Designed by Guy Callaby
Printed in the Czech Republic

Quiller
An imprint of Quiller Publishing Ltd
Wykey House, Wykey, Shrewsbury SY4 1JA
Tel: 01939 261616 Fax: 01939 261606
E-mail: info@quillerbooks.com
Website: www.quillerpublishing.com

# Drink!

*A seasonal selection of the best from* SPECTATOR

*by* **Bruce Anderson**

*Cartoons by* **Lachy Campbell**

Quiller

# ~ Contents ~

*Foreword by The Rt Hon David Cameron*     **8**

*Introduction*     **10**

● Searching for God in the twilight on the Aegean Sea     **13**

● Tradition and terroir: the new reign in Spain is producing great results     **15**

● London's perfect Paris brasserie     **17**

● Put your trust in Hungarian wine (yes, really)     **19**

● Too much too young: allow some wines to sleep long and peacefully     **21**

● Big two-hearted river: the wines of the Rhône     **23**

● Kilchoman isn't a good whisky; it's a great one     **25**

● I'm grateful for my grateful drinking friend     **27**

● Is the great vintage of 2015 retreating into itself?     **29**

● A Dutch treat from Bordeaux     **31**

● All's fair in love, Waugh and wine     **35**

● Thank Evans for Quintessentially good wine     **37**

● The king of clubs is a romantic at heart     **39**

● A toast to unsung heroes, the god of battles and the infinite desert stars  **41**

● The charms of old Paris and the naughtiest girl of the 20th century  **43**

● Burgundies that taste of T.S. Eliot  **45**

● From kittens to claret: an ideal education  **47**

● Bloody Marys and the funniest woman in the House of Lords  **49**

● The only good thing about the Soviet Union was cheap caviar  **53**

● What wine is worthy of white truffle? It took us a few tries to be sure  **55**

● Should NATO have embraced Russia?  **57**

● With great wine comes great anxiety  **59**

● The no-nonsense greatness of Australian wine  **61**

● Wine, women and willow: a perfect combo for a perfect English summer day  **63**

● Adventures of a hell-cat in heaven  **65**

● On the trail of a Burgundian Holy Grail  **69**

● A thirst for justice: the wit and wisdom of Oliver Wendell Holmes  **71**

● Wine merchants might just be the happiest people in the world  **73**

● The Society of Odd Bottles and the Sisterhood of the Black Pudding  **75**

● A toast to all bottles  **77**

● When it comes to food and wine, there's no place like Rhône  **79**

● The joy of Glenmorangie     **81**

● The soul of a lurcher and the secret of a capon     **83**

● Life and death of a Tokay     **85**

● Flowers of Scotland     **87**

● What it's like to drink a 118-year-old wine     **89**

● Dining in style at David Cameron's favourite Italian     **93**

● Enjoying South Africa's secret French connection     **95**

● When an economist turns into a winemaker     **97**

● When Glyndebourne is the most perfect place on earth     **99**

● Mourning Julia Gillard with the greatest wine ever to come out of Australia     **101**

● A lord's prayer     **103**

● The tastes of temptation     **105**

● Horse and bourbon     **107**

● Off the wagon     **109**

● Waters of life     **111**

● Progress in a bottle     **113**

● Queen of Burgundy     **115**

● Mature consideration     **117**

● Clubbable bottles     **119**

● Stars by any other name     **121**

● The single European goose     **123**

'What with the beret and the Breton jumper, I think Gerald might just be getting a little carried away with the whole home-grown wine effort!'

# ~ *Foreword* ~

Anyone who has had lunch with Bruce Anderson could be forgiven for thinking that the big man's interest in wine was about quantity, not quality. They would be wrong. While Anderson lunches – particularly in the 1990s – would often involve him ordering and opening four bottles of wine even before the first one was finished, his knowledge of what he was drinking was always second to none.

And he has never been one of those wine snobs who focus only on France. He would scour wine lists (and your cellar, if you had one) for interesting pinots, rieslings and grenaches from around the world.

On a brief tour of southern Spain he ordered the oldest and most obscure Riojas he could find. One was brown and full of sediment but he pressed on, instructing me to close my eyes and focus on the flavour.

While legendary for vast expenses claims that have tested the patience of newspaper editors for the last four decades, Bruce could always spot a bargain. I recall one lunch where a restaurant had mispriced some '82 Pomerol and he refused to leave until we had finished the entire stock.

Bruce's Speccie columns are a great mix of wine, politics, gossip and wisdom. I first met him when he stood in for Sir John Junor who wrote a column for the *Mail on Sunday*. As a young researcher at Conservative Central Office I used to feed the legendary Junor with tidbits, mostly about Labour splits. In turn, he would feed me with lunch in Kensington High Street where the conversation was all one way: his stories about dealing with Beaverbrook and his undying love for Princess Diana, Margaret Thatcher and, intriguingly, Selina Scott.

After a week Bruce concluded that I was 'marginally less useless than the rest of Smith Square' and so our friendship began.

Bruce is a forest of contradictions. A student Marxist who became a committed Conservative. A harsh critic one minute and a passionate supporter the next. A political obsessive and street fighter but with a hinterland that includes a knowledge of music, opera, art and theatre that is hard to beat.

Bruce has written and said things that put your teeth on edge (and that's putting it mildly), but you're never bored reading his columns or hearing his stories.

His wine columns are one of the things that makes the Speccie unmissable reading – and bringing them together in one place is long overdue. Not least because his friends can now access the Anderson wisdom on wine without jeopardising what's left of their livers.

**The Rt Hon David Cameron**

# ~ *Introduction* ~

Mary Queen of Scots had four Marys. *The Spectator* only has two, but at least neither is likely to be put to death. There is Dear Mary, that wry and sardonic counsellor. No-one since Jeeves has been so adept at navigating through the shoals of social embarrassment. The other is Mary Wakefield, who is a cross between Gerard Manley Hopkins — 'All things counter, original, spare, strange' — and Little Gidding. She seems wholly suited to a Dearly Beloved, via media Anglicanism, redolent of scholar gentlemen doing good works in country parishes while also acting as beacons of humane studies and, of course, basing their services on 1611 and 1662. Her debut in *The Spectator* was an arabesque of delicious reportage about a different sort of service. It took place in Holy Trinity Brompton, where there was a sermon about hamsters while yuppies serenaded God to the raucousness of electric guitars. Her gentle, more-in-sorrow-than-in-anger prose only highlighted the comprehensiveness of the intellectual filleting. Yet Mary has left for Rome, relieved that she no longer has to worry about the Church of England. Were I an Anglican, I would regard her departure as a grievous loss. The salt is losing its savour.

She is also responsible for all this. Around a decade ago, she decided that I should write a wine column for *The Spectator*. I protested that I knew nothing about wine. She demurred. A demurral from Mary is a formidable experience. She is not exactly Eve or Delilah. Nor is she Beatrice, or Violet Elizabeth Bott. As a literary model, it is more a matter of Elizabeth Bennet. But she knows how to get her way. I insisted that on wine, although I might have acquired a certain amount of bottle-learning, I had little book learning. Nor do I have an expert palate. She brushed all that aside. We agreed that the column should be entitled 'Drink' rather than merely wine, and that I should weave in other topics. I do not think that either of us realised just how far that warp and weft would reach.

Anyway, it was her idea. She is to blame, or even, perhaps, praise. With the exception of that two-hours-before-the-deadline moment, known to all hacks, when everything seems dark and doubtful, it has been fun to write. Somehow, the darkness always dispels. I hope it has also been fun to read.

**Bruce Anderson**

# ~ Searching for God in the twilight
# on the Aegean Sea ~

My friend Jonathan Gaisman recently gave rise to a profound philosophical question concerning wine. Jonathan is formidably clever. He has a tremendous reputation at the Commercial Bar. Although he brushes aside any compliments from the unqualified, there was a recent case — Excalibur — where his performance won the awed approval of lawyers to whom even he might concede quasi-peer status. They aver that his preparation was exemplary, his cross-examination ruthless and relentless; his triumph total.

That said, he is anything but a monoglot lawyer. Not only a music lover but a musicologist, modesty alone would prevent him from claiming that *Nihil artium a me alienum*. Among the minor arts, he is a practised oenologist. But he is also thoughtful and combative on the subject of religion, on which he and I have had many exchanges. In a recent issue of *Standpoint*, he wrote an essay, 'The devout sceptic', which came close to convincing this devout atheist. Almost thou persuadest me to be a Christian.

Almost, but there is a basic problem. It is not clear to me that Jonathan himself is a Christian. I have argued that no one can call himself a Christian unless he believes not only in the Incarnation but also in the literal truth of the Resurrection. If it is not true Christ died on the cross and was raised from the dead, Christianity is meaningless. This point irritates Jonathan. He does not see why I should prescribe rules for a club to which I do not belong. But I would retort that without the Resurrection, his version of Christianity has no theology and no historical continuity. It is merely a matter of aesthetics and ethical aspirations.

Jonathan once asked me whether I believed that there were mystical truths. Caught off intellectual balance, I replied: 'No'. I am still trying to decide whether I agree with myself. "'What is truth?" said jesting Pilate, and would not stay for an answer.' 'It depends what you mean by truth,' C.E.M. Joad would have asserted. I will be temerarious enough to assert that truth is only a useful concept if it relates to a subject matter that is verifiable. So mysticism may be beautiful. That does not make it truthful.

It is so tempting to conflate truth and beauty. Titian's *Assumption* in the Frari, the Mass in B Minor, Durham Cathedral. Surely none of them could have been created without faith. As one's soul soars in response to their sublimity, it seems churlish not to genuflect to that faith.

I cannot take that step. Man needs God, to make sense of the universe and his own existence. We find it impossible to accept that the universe is just an accident. But the need for God does not prove that He exists. It may be that we are adrift in a meaningless cosmos, condemned to a destiny of mini-tragic heroism in our own lives, with only stoicism to replace faith. If so, let us embrace stoicism and defy tragedy.

Recently, Jonathan had what should have been a most unstoical experience. He was off to the Aegean, on a yacht which was plentifully supplied with Château Pétrus. But he announced that he would drink only retsina. Was this a penitential exercise, perhaps expiating the massacre of an excessive number of solicitors? 'No,' he insisted. It was all about genius loci. I find that wholly incredible. Certainly, one would not wish to drink Pétrus — or any red wine — in the midday heat. But as the sun sets over the wine-dark sea, becoming God-haunted with nightfall so that one could easily imagine the Homeric deities setting forth from Mount Olympus to reclaim their dominions, what better than a beaker or two of Pétrus? Jonathan believes that God is everywhere. I think, with more evidence, that the same is true of Pétrus. That wine, in that sea: almost enough to make me a mystic.

# ~ Tradition and terroir: the new reign in Spain is producing great results ~

The Kingdom of Spain always sends outstanding ambassadors to the Court of St James's, and none more so than the appropriately named Santiago de Mora–Figueroa, Marqués de Tamarón, who was en poste when José María Aznar was the Spanish premier. Santiago is also a highly regarded poet, and he has a further advantage. He looks like a Grandee of Spain as painted by Velázquez or Goya. So during one of his recent visits, a good audience assembled to hear him.

There was an obvious agenda: Catalonia, the closely fought left/right conflict in Spanish politics, and Spanish attitudes to Brexit.

We took wit and charm for granted, while awaiting enlightenment and controversy. We waited in vain. All diplomats need to be able to play the forward defensive stroke but no one has ever deployed that essentially negative tactic more stylishly than Santiago. He said nothing that could have embarrassed the current ambassador or the Spanish government. Indeed, he said nothing at all. It was masterly.

The Tamarón family still owns the castle at Arcos de la Frontera, which they captured from the Moors during the Reconquista. The evening's chairman, Ignacio Peyró of the Instituto Cervantes (Spain's equivalent of the British Council), also has links with the Reconquista. His family comes from León, that ancient mountain kingdom which kept Spanishness alive under the Visigoths and the Umayyads, and which is on the pilgrim route to Compostela. In some places, León has a bleak landscape: baking rock below, a pitiless sun above. This has bred a wiry race of men, accustomed to adversity. Formidable fighters, they are easier to manage on the battlefield than on the parade ground. But there is also good agriculture, including viniculture.

Ignacio Peyró's family has an interest in Losada, a fascinating winery near Bierzo, a village not far from Compostela, and the centre of an ancient wine-growing region. Like the rest of Spanish winemaking, it has benefited from the economic modernisation that began under Franco but has gained momentum in recent decades: the EU has been good for Spain.

Like a lot of the best new winemakers, those in charge of Losada believe in the strengths of terroir and tradition, based on the mencía grape, which had been cultivated since the Middle Ages. The chief vigneron, Amancio Fernández, has no desire to work anywhere else: no other aim than to make the best possible wine in his native village.

He and the other new owners began with an innovation. Other wineries in the region had sought out slate slopes, in the expectation that this would enhance their wines' minerality. They were no doubt thinking of the limestone slopes of Burgundy and the glorious grapes which they produce. Losada went for old plots of mencía that had been forgotten or abandoned. Frequently, these were on clay soil. But there has been no loss of structure. I tasted the Pájaro Rojo, which was a sound table wine, but also the Losada and the Altos de Losada. Both of those had spent nine or ten months in French oak barrels: neither was over-oaked.

The Altos has complexity and had a satisfyingly long finish. I drank the '15, which benefits from some old vines which Losada has put back into commission. It was just about ready but has plenty more to say for itself. It will keep for at least a decade. At Losada, they are happy to insist that they are still studying their craft and working out how to raise their game. With the Altos, I think that they already have. I had recently introduced Ignacio to haggis. He had enjoyed it, naturally.

We agreed that the Losada wines would be a fine accompaniment: León rampant.

# ~ London's perfect Paris brasserie ~

We order some French things better in London — often, admittedly, with French help. A *grenouille* friend recently took me to lunch at the Beaujolais Club just off Charing Cross Road. He said that it overwhelmed him with nostalgia. As a child, living in Paris, if the family was in town for the weekend, it was just the sort of brasserie in which they would have Sunday lunch (cook's day off). Traditional dishes; proper bourgeois cooking; wine, no premiers crus, but solid, dependable bottles from solid, dependable growers — who were often friends or relatives of the owners. The children demonstrated their command of table manners and served an apprenticeship in gastronomy.

In Paris these days, such places are harder to find. Sometimes, the proprietors have been seduced by vaulting ambition and tried an Icarus-style ascent towards Michelin stardom. There is also the problem of the 35-hour week and women's emancipation. Good old Gaston, *le patron*, can no longer conscript his daughters and daughters-in-law in the way that his wife and previous female generations took for granted that they would pride themselves on serving a nation which has always marched on its stomach.

Moreover, the Parisian customer has often succumbed to the lure of trendiness and become an Athenian. To paraphrase: they spend their time in nothing else, but to eat some new thing. The culinary apostolic succession from *grand-mère* and the generations before her is scorned. There are new customers, but some of them are Americans, suspicious of foreign cooking and inclined to regard a single glass of wine as enough for a family of four.

This all helps to explain why Jean-Yves, maître de Beaujolais, who hails from the Breton-Norman marches, is glad to be working in London. Even so, there is absolutely no derogation from Frenchness. You eat *chez* Marianne. The dishes may vary from day to day, yet there is a dependable sameness. Though Jean-Yves can produce serious bottles, principally from the Rhône, there is no great wine. But everything is reliable and reasonably priced. We started with a Montlouis from Jacky Blot, an outstanding vigneron. It was almost mouth-puckeringly dry. A fine aperitif, it would work well with smoked fish. The list has no bargains, but there is nothing to deter the ordering of the third bottle.

The waitresses are equally French and instantly identifiable as such. With subtle, wry faces, plus a hint of the serene secrecy of an international Gothic Virgin, their demeanour towards their customers is a gracious welcome spiked with a touch of sardonic amusement. There is a blend of antecedent suffering quotient and joyousness to come. They remind one of actresses in those splendid modern French films: *Le Placard*, *Le Dîner de Cons*, et al.

All that said, there is one respect in which Beaujolais does fly very high. Its cheese board is an epitome of French civilisation. I do not believe that the French have a monopoly on cheese-mongering genius. Stilton is up there, as long as it is unpasteurised. Otherwise, go for Stichelton from next door, which cannot call itself Stilton but is made from raw milk. Above all, there is proper gorgonzola: raw milk, cheese mites — ambrosial.

But for the sheer volume of serious cheese, France is unsurpassable, as Beaujolais demonstrates. I do know of one better cheese board in London, at the Gavroche. It is somewhat more expensive. Moreover, it tolerates non-French cheeses. Without being ultra-Gallican in nationalism, Beaujolais would sound the toxin: '*à table, citoyens ... qu'un fromage impur abreuve nos sillons.*' Needless to say, we finished with Calvados. It was altogether an excellent repast: perfect for a non-dieting day.

# ~ Put your trust in Hungarian wine (yes, really) ~

The wines of Tokaji run like a golden thread through Hungarian history. There are references to their nectar-like quality in the Hungarian national anthem. Imperial Tokaji, the world's sweetest wine, has always been prized. As its name implies, much of it found its way to the Habsburgs' cellars. Emperors often used it as birthday or Christmas presents for fellow monarchs. So I was delighted to taste some non-imperial bottles over dinner at the Hungarian embassy, courtesy of that impressive fellow Kristóf Szalay-Bobrovniczky, the ambassador, a good friend of Prime Minister Orbán's. Mr Orbán is much demonised. Along with President Trump and Brexit, he is seen to be a threat to the Fifth International: the pseudo-liberal bureaucratic one. That apart, he cannot be accused of resembling Mr Trump.

At times, Hungarian democracy may have a rough edge: can anyone name a single infant democracy in which that was not the case? From the Turkish victory at Mohács to the glorious uprising in 1956 — and beyond — Hungary was often embattled and frequently oppressed. Those are not the easiest circumstances for cultivating the gentler arts of government. Moreover, Mr Orbán is a patriot and a Christian: how deeply unfashionable. He believes Hungary should control its own borders: how un-European. Having escaped Soviet rule, he is not interested in being told what to do by the Germans. How absurd: does he not realise that it is more than 70 years since the Germans tried to exterminate anyone? Does he not trust the Bundesreich?

It was certainly easy to trust the Hungarian wines. The sweet wines — aszú — are the product of dried grapes which have developed noble rot and are harvested as late as January. They are grown on a plateau full of extinct volcanoes. Broken-down igneous rock has infused the soil with a steely minerality, of particular assistance to the furmint grape, which is used for the aszú wines but also bottled on its own. I was especially impressed by a 2011 Palandor from the Karádi-Berger winery. Crisp but also subtle and with plenty of length, it would work well as an aperitif or with smoked fish; think of it as filling the role of a fino or a dry white Bordeaux.

The aszú wines have further to go. Production standards fell away under the communists and though the recovery has been enthusiastic, it is still incomplete. Tokaji makers tend to be patronising about Sauternes or Barsac, insisting that their vineyards are much older. Be that as it may, the Magyars have not yet succeeded in emulating the spine of structure which we find in the finest sweet Bordeaux. In some ways, that is strange. Good furmint has plenty of structure. Given a bit more time, the vignerons will surely succeed in passing that on to the aszú bottles. But good Hungarian wine is good value. Look out for the Royal Tokaji label and prepare to salute a work in progress.

Sweetness: on Sunday, I lunched with an old friend at Scalini in Fulham. Italian by name and by nature, at least during weekends; this would not be the ideal place for a business lunch, but who wants to talk business over Sunday lunch? The place was full of Italian families. Why is it that in restaurants, their children, though not in the least repressed, seem to have a lesser share of original sin than their English equivalents? While smiling at their innocence, there was plenty to encourage pleasantly sinful thoughts. In response to summer weather, the place could have been rechristened *all'ombra delle ragazze in fiore*. These *ragazze* were fetching enough to remind one of the Tenth Commandment: 'Thou shalt not covet thy neighbour's ass.' Inter alia we drank a good Gavi — Broglia 2016 — which did nothing to discourage ... seasonal thoughts.

# ~ Too much too young: allow some wines to sleep long and peacefully ~

This April is the cruellest month, but not in the sense that Eliot intended. Memory and desire are mixed: memory for previous verdant seasons; aching desire for a new one. Instead, we appear to have permanent midwinter spring, with the emphasis on midwinter.

So this might seem to be absolutely the wrong time to drink rosé. Readers may be aware of my considered prejudice, that rosé works well south of Lyon as a wine to drink mid-morning with the last crumbs of croissant. But there is the Domaines Ott, whose pretensions and prices soar well above the ground level of normal Provençal plonk. I had some the other day, in the most depressing environment possible. 'The doors clap to, the pane is blind with showers.' It was as if the elements were sneering: 'You dare to drink rosé, in early April, in England? We'll learn you.'

The lesson failed. Clos Mireille, from Ott, was a prejudice diffuser. By any standards, this is a serious wine. It has plenty of fruit, but also structure and length. I drank a 2016. Though we were stopping short of infanticide, the wine was barely ready. I would like to taste it in future years, for the evolution will be interesting. As a food companion, it will stand up to something a lot more serious than croissant shards.

Youth and evolution: I have been hearing a lot lately about the 2005 clarets. There seems to be a consensus that anything much above Cru Bourgeois is too young to drink, and that to be ready for dinner, even the minor wines need decanting at breakfast. That said, there is no anxiety among the experts. A lot of the 1975s went from extreme youth to extreme old age without an intervening phase. No one thinks that the 2005s will suffer a similar fate. They are merely sleeping peacefully and will awaken joyfully. But they are not yet ready for a fairy prince with a corkscrew.

This was especially true of the Bahans Haut-Brion, as the second wine of Haut-Brion used to be named, until it was re-christened Le Clarence de Haut-Brion, after the great Clarence Dillon. I remember tasting the '05 in 2010, and deciding it was full of promise but needed another five years. It was already depressingly expensive. Last week, the promise was even more apparent, as was the need for time, as was the expense. The Bahans had been opened for two hours: not nearly long enough. It still needs another five years. And as for price: approaching £1,000 a case if you can find it.

Prices of that magnitude raise a philosophical question, hitherto avoided in this column. At what point does it become absurd to spend a lot of money on a case of wine? Suppose the alternative were a weekend in Venice, or a painting? Surely either would be preferable? I am told that because of the idleness of the modern housewife, addicted to her dishwasher, a late 18th-century Coalport dinner service is now as cheap as chips. How much wine would one of those be worth? There are two answers to that question. The first is tough-minded and sounds philistine: it depends on how rich you are. The second opens the casement to romanticism. We should not under-estimate the cultural potency of a great wine. I have just helped to drink a 1995 Léoville Barton. A bottle like that trails clouds of glory. It acts as a communion wine, consecrating a mystical union between the drinkers and old high European civilisation.

There is one way of avoiding the relative value question: find good wines from a lesser year. I have been lucky enough to drink a number of 2004s recently. None disappointed. The Léoville Barton, the Pontet-Canet and the Batailley were excellent. Lesser names, jolly good — and they were all ready. To conclude: Domaines Ott in anticipation of summer — proper claret as a consolation for the season's delay.

# ~ Big two-hearted river: the wines of the Rhône ~

The Rhône is a strong river. The Loire derives graciousness from its châteaux. The Rhine and the Thames have been sentimentalised: not the Rhône. There are no Rhône-maidens, no suggestion of 'sweet Rhône run softly till I end my song'. A powerful onrush of water rips past the banks of a river that knows how to drown men.

But it also brings fertility in abundance. This is probably the oldest wine-growing region in France. The romantic version is that Greeks brought the Shiraz grape from Persia; 2,500 years later, syrah is still the region's vinous bedrock. As one would expect from a combination of the River God and the Sun God, these are powerful wines, easily hitting 14 degrees. Even Hemingway declared that Châteauneuf is not a lunchtime wine.

Single bottles are always a temptation. All too often, it is one that should be resisted. Great wine needs a lengthy and untroubled maturation. It should be put to sleep like Brünnhilde, until a hero arrives for the awakening. If the bottle has been forgotten about and bundled around in various house-movings before coming to rest next to the central heating boiler, the owners will end up with a somewhat ill-tempered Valkyrie.

My experiment took place in the early 1980s. There were no heroes or dragons: merely a wine merchant who had three bottles of Hermitage from the 1920s. He offered no guarantee about their condition. To adopt the booksellers' idiom, they were for sale 'with all faults'. I cannot remember the price. It was cheap if the bottles had retained their quality: not so, if they had turned to vinegar. It would be unfair to describe the first two as vinegar: unfair on vinegar. They smelt as if they might be a substitute for Novichok. But the third, a 1929, was Apollonian: one of the greatest wines I have tasted and a hero that any Valkyrie would be happy to carry to Valhalla. My friend John Beveridge has described the '67 Yquem as 'like a Greek temple melted down in honey'. That Hermitage deserved a similar tribute.

Over the weekend, when the hostess could spare time from discussing the arrangements for Monday's meet, we were discussing Rhône-ish matters in Dorset. In geography and climate, the two regions may be dissimilar, but in zest for life there could be an unending and friendly rivalry. In both of them, agriculture is central. In both cases, the craft and husbandry associated with cultivation produces proper people. Dorset has its grand families but — perhaps to a greater extent than in any other English county — there is also a backbone of yeomanry. In all this, hunting is crucial. The hunting field is a classic Burkean coalition: the dead, the living and the yet unborn. That there are people wicked enough to wish to eradicate this more-than sport — this almost mystic affirmation of England and its people — demonstrates the extent to which the left is in the grip of malignancy and psychosis: of hatred for the country which it wishes to dominate. We must save hunting for the as yet unborn.

There are areas in which Dorset must give best. So we turned to the Rhône for wine. My friends produced their last two bottles of Château de Beaucastel 2000. It is a superb wine, made by the Perrin family, who blend every one of the 13 Rhône grape varietals. The wine was ready, but there is still plenty of life. If you are fortunate enough to own some, there need be no hurry to finish it off. Its second wine, Coudoulet de Beaucastel, is also admirable. What the Perrins do not know about viniculture is not knowledge.

Recently, I have been drinking a certain amount of Cornas, while resolving to increase the tempo. One of the smallest Rhône appellations and using only syrah, it produces sophisticated and long-lived bottles. So we toasted its success and hunting's survival.

# ~ Kilchoman isn't a good whisky; it's a great one ~

'What seas what shores what grey rocks … / What water lapping the bow.' So evocative, which seems strange: one would have assumed that Eliot would have been seasick crossing the Channel. Yet he understood the gentle little tides — and also the beauty and the fear, the other-worldliness, the implacable grandeur, of the great waters' vast dominions. In these islands, throughout the centuries, men have earned their bread from the sea. But it was rarely an easy harvest. The Mingulay Boat Song captures the perils of the quest. 'When the wind is wild with shouting / And the waves mount ever higher / Anxious eyes turn ever seaward / Wives are waiting, since break of day / To see us home, boys, to Mingulay.' Not all those boys made it home.

I was thinking of this while drinking Kilchoman whisky, Gaelic Scotland's latest gift to civilisation. On the island of Islay is Machir Bay, one of the most beautiful beaches in the United Kingdom. The scenery is superb, the water enticing and, apart from seabirds' cries, it is usually deserted: the sort of place where you feel resentful if the binoculars pick out another picnicker. A beautiful day in May: turquoise water; irresistible. Divest yourself of clothing, run in, keep running — bloody hell, where is the Gulf Stream when you need it? A brief immersion, then rush out and glory in the invigoration, especially if you have packed a hip flask.

In future the beach may not be so empty. Half a mile away there is a distillery, which produces Kilchoman. It was established by Anthony Wills of the Bristol tobacco family. With such a pedigree, it was natural that his commercial horizons should lie to the West, especially as his wife's family came from Islay. Magnetic pull, mysticism, tradition — were all reinforced by technique.

The mightiest Islay whiskies have always had peat at their core. It might seem excessive to compare this to the fugal passage in the slow movement of Eroica, the greatest symphonic music of all, but I remember drinking an ancient Ardbeg, than which there is no finer whisky, with the windows open to the West and Ultima Thule, to that accompaniment. It was as if the two artworks were saluting one another, like the flagships of allied powers, in the days when those vessels would have been 40,000-ton battleships.

Peat is not to every taste, especially when accompanied by strong notes of iodine and seaweed. A few years ago, bad times struck and Ardbeg itself was mothballed (there is a horrifying parallel with the Royal Navy's current impoverishment). But matters have improved. The whisky market has expanded and peat is back in fashion. Ardbeg is once again resplendent; there is talk of recommissioning long-defunct distilleries and Kilchoman has been launched to general acclaim: the first new distillery on Islay for 124 years. The Willses knew what they wanted to achieve: a harmony of peat and sweetness. So they use bourbon and oloroso barrels to ensure lighter, fruity notes, while also malting most of their own barley at Rockside Farm.

I tried their Machir Bay, the most generally available, and was immensely impressed, especially when I learned that it was only six years old. Whisky only ages in barrels, and malts are normally reckoned to require at least ten years. That has an obvious drawback: ten years is a long time to wait for cash flow. But Kilchoman seems to have found an answer. As they are already winning golden opinions while producing only 200,000 litres a year, it is to be hoped that they will hold back a few barrels to see how it matures.

I ought to introduce a note of caution because I drank it after a good dinner. Even so, I am confident that Kilchoman is not a good whisky. It is a great whisky: a magnificent addition to the symphony of Scottish malts. It is pleasant to note that something is going well in the world.

## ~ I'm grateful for my grateful drinking friend ~

The phone rang. 'You are the last person in the world I should be talking to,' proclaimed an old friend from the States. 'How have I offended you this time?' was my surprised reply. 'Not you personally. My beef is with your hero Donald Trump.' 'That is not true. In any jurisdiction, I always like to support the most right-wing legal party, so I keep on hoping that the President will calm down and stop tweeting. Then one could relax and enjoy his capacity to infuriate whining leftist belly-achers. But he is devaluing his office and demeaning the great republic: no hero of mine.'

'Oh well, I forgive you and anyway I need your help, on Rousseau.' 'I'm not sure I've much to offer. My reading of Rousseau is incomplete and out of date. I did conclude that the General Will was a dangerous concept, easily adaptable by totalitarians who wanted a justification for keeping mankind in chains. In private life, he was a profoundly selfish fellow: a blend of Donald Trump and Boris Johnson. Anyway ...'

'Not Jean-Jacques, for God's sake. Armand.' 'Now you're talking.' The house of Armand Rousseau produces great Burgundy. I have not drunk enough of their bottles to feel able to pronounce. But some of those who enjoy that great fortune would insist that there is no finer grower of pinot noir. Armand himself, the founder, sounds to have been a character out of Balzac, but one with an instinctive understanding of Burgundy. He was forever buying little parcels of land, seeing potential previous owners had overlooked. Today, the family has 30 acres of vines, half of them producing grands crus. Armand was killed in a car crash coming back from hunting (sanglier rather than fox) but not before he had created a formidable inheritance.

His son Charles and grandson Eric have maintained dynastic momentum. Eric, an oenologue as well as an oenophile, has a fine collection of degrees and diplomas: science in the service of tradition and terroir. I know that my American friend does everything possible to ingratiate himself with those who might be selling Rousseaus. He takes delight in such purchases. Around the beginning of the century, before I knew him so well, I had heard about a considerable cellar which was available for a discreet sale, probably in three lots. I mentioned it over dinner in his presence. I had not realised a) how rich he was and b) that when it comes to serious wine, he is the opposite of risk averse. So a casual piece of information led to an eagle's swoop of a purchase, completed by mid-morning the next day. He bought the lot. I was worried that he had spent too much: shows how good I am at reading markets. The surviving bottles are worth several times what he paid for everything. More to the point, he feels that he owes me a debt of gratitude.

Now, he wanted to assess the progress of more recent acquisitions: some Rousseaus (he keeps one of his cellars in London). There were three of us for five bottles, over a simple repast: jamon; English ham whose succulence was an attractive contrast to the Spaniard's austere power; cold roast mutton, and a bit of chèvre. We began with three wines from Clos de la Roche: '07, '08 and '12. I counselled against opening the youngster: correctly. Although there was considerable promise, it was some way from being ready. A third of the bottle survived until lunch the next day and was said to have opened out. It needs five years. The other two were barely ready, even after three hours in the decanter. Both were splendid. My vote went to the '08, but not by much.

We moved onwards to grandeur. A 2002 Clos St Jacques was as good a bottle of Burgundy as I had drunk for some years. But it was eclipsed by a Chambertin Clos de Bèze of the same vintage. Magnificent on the nose, it had everything: subtlety, power, length, majesty, harmony. I have never drunk a finer Burgundy. I resolved to cultivate my friend's sense of gratitude.

## ~ Is the great vintage of 2015
retreating into itself? ~

We were pondering the relationship between military history and wine vintages. It is extraordinary to think that the French managed to make wine throughout both world wars. In the late 1980s, Alan Clark had David Owen and me to lunch at Saltwood, his castle near Hythe. It is a proper castle; the stones are still marked by the rust of medieval warfare. According to legend, the knights who slew Thomas à Becket made their final preparations there. How appropriate for a future Clark residence. There was some dispute as to whether Alan went over to Rome on his deathbed, but during the years of swaggering health his sympathies would have been with the swordsmen, not the croziers. He would have had little use for turbulent priests.

Anyway, he produced a swagger wine. In the diaries, he claims that it was a 1916 Latour. Agreeing about the year, I am certain that it was a La Mission Haut-Brion. 'This should be fine,' declared our host. 'I opened it two hours ago.' I said nothing but feared greatly. With a wine three-quarters of a century old, it is wiser to uncork and pour. There is an analogy with opening an ancient tomb. Occasionally, miraculously, the corpse has been preserved. Then the fresh air arrives and it crumbles into dust.

Alan's wine did not crumble. Over the hill, yes, but it had been a very high hill. There was still plenty of fruit as well as tannin. We wondered how it would have been harvested and bottled. Although Bordeaux was not within shelling range of the Western Front, it would have fallen under the shadow, like the whole of France. Young able-bodied men would have been long gone: some no doubt already fallen; more about to be claimed in the defence of Verdun. For replacements: females, boys, *vieillards* — also, no doubt, some *mutilés de guerre*. All of them embodying the spirit of '*ils ne passeront pas*'. By the time we drank their bottle, almost all would have passed on, but we complimented their shades for producing a wine of such enduring substance.

A hundred years after Verdun, the Burgundy weather tried to equal the worst climatic horrors of Flanders warfare. An inundation of rain was followed by a frost in late April. Some vineyards almost gave up. It is a tribute to modern vinicultural techniques, not to mention grit and determination worthy of Pétain's *poilus*, that any grapes survived. With the help of late sunshine, they did, though yields were drastically reduced.

This is one reason why the vintage is underrated. Another is its proximity to the 2015; big wines, full of fruit but disciplined by tannin. Bottles like that can suck the oxygen out of the market. The '15s have distracted attention from both the '16s and the '14s.

I wonder. There is no doubt that 2015 was a great year. The experts are unanimous. Yet the surrounding years should not be underrated. Moreover, the '14s are already drinkable, even premiers crus. It would be a shame to overindulge in bottles that have a fascinating maturation ahead of them: the best ones will last until the 2030s. But reports from the tasting frontline suggest that the 2015s have retreated into themselves. This is not unknown among serious wines. In earlier years, it was true of some of the '82 clarets. There is every reason to expect a second coming. Even so, I still harbour doubts. I wonder if some of the wines will eventually turn out to have too much fruit, making harmony impossible to achieve.

As for the '16s, anything from Domaine des Lambrays or Albert Bichot will be outstanding, and priced accordingly. At a recent tasting, Bichot's Chambertin was beyond praise. In all this, we are dealing with biology, climate and humanity. What an endlessly fascinating study, especially when wine is the end product.

# ~ A Dutch treat from Bordeaux ~

In 1995, a young Dutchman completed an MBA. Banking beckoned. An internship was arranged. But Alexander van Beek thought that he would have a brief gap-summer before surrendering to a life of suited servitude in a counting house. Even though he spoke no French and had little technical knowledge of wine, he went to Bordeaux, rocked up at Château Giscours and asked for a job.

Several points were in his favour. He worked hard and never minded getting his hands muddy. He cheerfully put up with any amount of teasing, which encouraged him to learn enough French to fire back. Finally, Giscours and its neighbour du Tertre had been bought by a Dutch family, who were not thrown by the idea of a fellow Dutchman becoming a vigneron. So the summer passed. Alexander stayed. And stayed, and stayed. The internship was held open. Perhaps it still is. It seems unlikely that it will be needed.

The early years were difficult. Giscours had been run down. Investment had been lacking and some of the vines had deteriorated. There were accusations that some of Giscours' second wine, Sirène, had been adulterated. It is also possible that the charges had been inspired by envy. The legal process dragged on for years and was never conclusively resolved. Anyone who doubts the absolute superiority of the English legal system to its French counterpart ought to examine the Sirène case.

Fortunately, the new owners were both rich and undeterred. They regarded their new venture as a labour of love. Alexander did a lot of the labour, and loved it. Long before he took command of the whole enterprise, he had won a formidable reputation in an industry which has never rushed to put foreign talent at its ease. Not that he has ever eschewed cosmopolitanism. Alexander runs one of the best cricket teams in Bordeaux and is even now trying to entice a young Englishman to sign up to the — wine — team. It is wholly irrelevant that the youth is also a promising all-rounder.

The other evening, some of us had the good fortune to admire the results of the van Beek stewardship, despite attempts at sabotage by man and nature. Another London tasting had been arranged, but the organisers backed out. They deserve to feel extremely foolish. Mark Walford, the intermediary, was busy with nature conservancy in the Highlands. A grouse moor is never an ideal location for complicated mobile-phone negotiations, and the French air traffic controllers were on strike. In the end, everything came together with the finesse and brio of the final paragraphs of a Jeeves and Wooster story.

Giscours is a third growth, du Tertre a fifth. Although this manifested itself, that was solely due to Giscours' excellence. We had the 2001 en magnum: superb claret in the prime of middle-aged maturity. The 2012, as one expected, was backward, but it is a wine of immense promise. The 2005 took the laurels. It was close to perfection.

The du Tertre wines were all excellent, but its 2012 was accessible now. That said, it will last. The 2000 was still batting like an accomplished stroke-player. In most other vinous company, du Tertre would have excelled. Yet there is no disgrace in being overshadowed by Giscours. In general, as Alexander put it, Giscours was the more intellectual of the two wines. This is his doing. Over the years, he has substantially increased the proportion of that most intellectual of grapes, cabernet sauvignon.

At the end of the evening, we gave Alexander a hearty send-off. Banking's loss was our gain.

'After a hard day's wine tasting,
so nice to get back home and break All the rules !'

# ~ All's fair in love, Waugh and wine ~

I was reminded of Wild West films from boyhood. Then, the beleaguered garrison scanned the horizon; would the US cavalry arrive in time to save them from being scalped? (John Wayne always did.) Now, one was hoping for relief, not from the Injuns, but in the form of an Indian summer. This is of especial interest to those who have a tendresse for Somerset cricket. Its paladins usually have a charmingly amateur quality. As Cardus wrote of an earlier cricketing vintage: '[They are] children of the sun and wind and grass. Nature fashioned them rather than artifice.' Somerset needs a match or two in order to gain points and avoid relegation. That said, the way we were playing earlier in the season, being rained off was the best hope.

It would help if those in charge of schedules should remember three things. County cricket is a summer game. It is also one of the glories of English civilisation, almost entitled to rank with the cathedrals and the common law. As such, it must not be brushed aside in the interests of junk sport, or whatever they call 20/20. But an ungenerous climate can bring consolations. That prince of foragers, young Louis, deciding that these were the perfect conditions for mushrooms, set off into the wood with a bucket and brought it back, full of chanterelles.

Scoffing them, we also drew on the lingering fruits of summer. A summer pudding was to be garnished with some final wild strawberries. They always look delicious — and the name. Caviar apart, is there anything more alluring in the culinary vocabulary? That said, what about the taste? In that passage of *Decline and Fall* so aptly named 'Pervigilium Veneris', Margot and Paul saunter from bed to lunch. In Waugh, low-life deflation is never far away. They come across Philbrick, that master of multi-faceted fraudulence, who is eating some of those 'bitter little strawberries which are so cheap in Provence and so very expensive in Dover Street.' He warns Paul that the League of Nations is taking a beady-eyed interest in Margot's business (the Mistress Quickly of 1920s Belgravia, she is the most elegant whore monger in all literature). 'Bitter' is surely an exaggeration, perhaps a deliberate one. Waugh may have intended to signal the bitter-sweet fate waiting in ambush for his principal characters. Yet he had a point. The tiny wild berries work as a heraldic escort to the taste-bud fireworks of British strawberries. On their own, they flatter to deceive.

In love and cookery, earthiness has an honoured place. The beef was roasting. To accompany it, Roland harvested some horseradish, mired in mud. There was then a problem. Our table was to be graced by a much greater power than horseradish, and the two must never be allowed to mingle. In decanters, the grandeur of earlier autumns awaited us. We stopped to sniff and stayed to genuflect.

I had warned my friends that luncheon would not only be an occasion for indulgence. There was work to be done. We had two bottles to compare, a 1989 and a 2000, both from that superb house Léoville Barton. The debate was vigorous, and inconclusive. The memsahib thought the '89 was just about the finest claret she had ever drunk, and one could taste why. A harmony of sun and nature and artifice, it was in a state of grace. So often when drinking such a wine, one wonders whether it would have benefited from another three years, or would have been even better three years earlier. This was perfect. The novice, the 2000, divided opinions. Still shy of 20, it was a young unbroken colt. Even so, I thought it deserved the blue riband.

What fun. Louis, his palate not yet trained to Bordeaux, but permitted a sip, began to understand why the grown-ups were so intent at the glass. The seasons, the generations, the wine: by the end, we could hear the music of the spheres.

# ~ Thank Evans for Quintessentially good wine ~

There was an entirely forgotten leftist called Allen Ginsberg, a so-called beat poet (surely an oxymoron) who once produced a work entitled 'Howl'. That was appropriate. It reads like a wolf on hallucinogens. The author whined that he had seen the best minds of his generation destroyed. 'Best minds': how would he have known? This was hardly Dunbar lamenting the makars of his era. Such of their verse that survives may now be an unyielding read. But in their day they were names to conjure with. Nor did they put their minds up their noses, or inject their hopes into ravaged veins.

I was thinking about poetry, decadence and self-destruction because I have decided that after a gap — horrifying thought — of 50 years, it is time to make a new assault on the French 19th century, before my *grenouille* rusts away completely. I revisited the Pleiades over the summer. Ronsard's enchantment is undimmed: his enthusiasm for carpe diem more relevant than ever — and my French can still cope with him. So what about moving on a few centuries to the harder task of Baudelaire et al?

Although they got up to some exotic carpe-ing in their diem, some of them do excite sympathy. One is Gérard de Nerval, who took a pet lobster for walks around the Palais-Royal, using a ribbon as a leash, and was promptly locked up in a madhouse. Poor fellow: in Paris of all places, what did he expect? Misusing a delicious crustacean, perhaps encouraging others to do likewise, thus undermining French gastronomy in the name of lobster liberation: he was probably better off in a fortified asylum, whose thick walls would protect him from the wrath of French gourmets.

Then there was Villiers de l'Isle-Adam, an unhappy member of a family of unhappy fantasists, all of them qualifying for the role of Prince à la Tour abolie. He is best known for 'Vivre? les serviteurs feront cela pour nous'. That reminded me of a recent discovery: a scintillating wine company called Quintessentially. It grew out of a concierge service of the same name, which ministers to the very rich. While it will not go so far as to do their living for them, it will provide its clients with everything that they request, though strictly within the law. Think of Jeeves, but without the note of disapproval when it comes to the young master's cravats. From the outset, wine was a crucial part of the service.

Then one of the wine experts decided to branch out, though the departure was amicable and the rich continue to benefit from his expertise. Even if born in Australia, Stevie Evans is a thoroughly civilised fellow, and a realistic one, entirely reconciled to England's upcoming triumph in the Ashes. His forebears cannot have been transported for anything too atrocious. Stevie loves wine. When he discusses his bottles, his eagerness effervesces. Wine and poetry march in step — and enthusiasm is matched by judgment.

Evans's Quintessentially Wine specialises in small parcels of good wine, impeccably sourced and ready for drinking now. That said, much of it will keep for years. Readers may be aware of my prejudices. A French friend always insists that I should learn the difference between oenophilia and necrophilia. I reply that when the wine deserves it, age should have an honoured place. I tried Stevie's Sena '15, which may be the best Chilean wine ever, and an Argentinian, Finca Piedra Infinita '13. Yes, they are drinking now, and would be ideal with bloody, well-hung beef. But they will last.

So will his La Fleur Morange '10, his Isole e Olena '14, and indeed his Cos d'Estournel 1990: no hurry to finish off such a fine vintage. But the stuff does not lurk around; there is hardly a gap between offer and sale. Quintessentially is not cheap. When it comes to fine wine, where is? Its acquaintance is worth making.

# ~ The king of clubs
# is a romantic at heart ~

We were discussing romanticism, with me arguing that it should be confined to the boudoir, the bedroom, the library or the stage. When it escapes into public affairs, disaster often ensues. This led to us reminiscing about romantics we had known, and one of our number denounced the late John Aspinall, who, he said, would have liked to pass as a romantic but was really a society card-sharp. The animus was understandable. This chap would have been significantly richer if his great-uncle had never found his way to Aspers's gaming tables. Aspers led on to Jimmy Goldsmith, undoubtedly a romantic and charismatic figure, but a consistent political menace — and thus to Jimmy's nephew by marriage, Robin Birley.

He is a romantic figure, straight out of Byron's 'Don Juan'. When he was still a schoolboy he was nearly killed by a tiger at John Aspinall's zoo. Aspers believed in recycling the plunder from card-sharping into the preservation of rare animals. Heedless of risk, he liked to disport himself with them and encouraged the zoo staff to do the same. That sometimes had consequences. The animals enjoyed the best of everything in the way of diet and could never have complained of hunger. This did not stop them having the odd chomp of keeper. Aspers's zoos were heavy on keepers.

One day, while Robin was in hospital recovering from the tiger's attentions — which needed several operations — a lawyer arrived at his bedside and started asking questions. Robin asked him what this was all about. 'Well, I'm gathering the details we'll need for the legal action against Mr Aspinall.' 'No you won't. There will be no action. What I did was my responsibility, not John Aspinall's.'

In one respect, Robin is very un-English. He is passionate about glamour, style, elegance. In an Englishman that would normally mean someone who danced at the wrong end of the ballroom: nothing like that about Robin. Glamour is in his lineage. His father, Mark, started Annabel's, while his grand-father Oswald was a good painter. He is often referred to as a society painter, but the stress should be on painter. Like James Gunn, he is currently underrated. Robin has already established one club, 5 Hertford Street, which has a chic reminiscent of Annabel's a generation ago, when it was known as Mabel's and seemed to be full of Guards officers and debutantes. These days it is being refurbished and its name will be broadcast in neon lights. That will disturb the nightingales in Berkeley Square.

Now he is expanding, with a new club in Albemarle Street to open in February, named Oswald's (the nickname will inevitably be Mosley's). Its main focus will be on wine. After a stiffish membership fee, patrons will be able to drink excellent bottles at retail prices, or bring their own with no corkage charge. If they have a case but only want to drink some of it, the club will sell the rest for them.

I was treated to the sort of bottles Oswald's might offer. We started with a Puligny-Montrachet Premier '13 Champs Canet from Domaine Jacques Carillon: excellent. Then the star, an '89 Léoville Barton: a superb wine of first-growth quality. Thank goodness I was not asked to identify the year, because I would have confidently plumped for 2000. Then we drank a '90 St Emilion, from a property that is no longer producing wine: Château Magdelaine. It was outshone by the Léoville Barton — but almost any other bottle would have been, too. In Oswald's, those clarets might sell for a little over £100 a bottle. These days, that is a bargain.

We finished off with a first-rate Calvados, the perfect accompaniment to a couple of cigars. Though the lunch may not have been a romantic experience, it was certainly a mellowing one.

# ~ A toast to unsung heroes, the god of battles and the infinite desert stars ~

We were talking about war, the desert and God. In the early seventies, one of our number, Christopher James, had been involved in serious fighting in the struggles to stop Yemeni-backed communist insurgents from destabilising Oman. Christopher was happy to pay tribute to everyone else, but evasive about his own service in the SAS. That savage little war of peace witnessed much unsung gallantry, not least by one of the most under-decorated soldiers in military history: Sgt Talaiasi Labalaba, also SAS. In 1972, he won a battle by firing a 25 pounder as if it had been a rifle (it normally needs a crew of three or four). Hit repeatedly, he persevered as if he had struck a deal with the god of battles: do not take me until the day is won. It was a clear VC. Because of political constraints, he ended up with a posthumous mention in dispatches. Somehow, that seems to symbolise the Heath government.

Christopher spent many a night under the desert stars, hundreds of miles from artificial light. He said that it felt like looking into the universe and that it commanded faith: a bleak and fierce monotheistic faith, which could easily accommodate a god of battles, but would have no use for polychrome statuary or intercessionary saints. 'Thou overmasters me, God! ... I kiss my hand to the stars.' In Christopher's judgment, you had to experience the god of the great desert to come to terms with Islam. Only then would you understand the frustration and the sense of inadequacy gnawing at many modern Muslims. They know how their faith was shaped; in austerity. Many of them find it easy to conclude that it has been squandered in fleshpots and whorehouses — Western whorehouses at that.

Although the desert has always spoken to a certain sort of British romantic, Christopher has spent his life wrestling with realpolitik. He knows that the two perspectives have to be harmonised. That is especially important in post-religious Britain, where there is an idle but widespread assumption that all grievances are either economic or incomprehensible. We could learn something from the brief history of modern Oman, where realpolitik was successfully deployed to ensure the survival of the monarchy, but where the sultan commissioned a new mosque, which is both magnificent and numinous. This was around the time that we celebrated two millennia of Christianity by building a hugely expensive dead insect: the 'Millennium Dumb'. The contrast is rage-making.

As well as toasting Labalaba, we commemorated a soldier and a statesman, Tim Landon, who played a crucial part in ensuring that Oman's victories in battle led to peacetime success. We had been given a bottle from his cellar. First, however, there were two contrasting Burgundies, both from the excellent Domaine de Montille. The first, a Volnay 1er Cru Les Mitans 2010, was voluptuous and feminine, like a line of sinuous dancers performing under the heavens in an oasis. The second, a Pommard Les Pézerolles 2009, also a 1er Cru, was massy and pugnacious, like a squadron of Challenger IIs accelerating into action. It got the early vote, but as the Volnay opened out, opinion was divided. Without losing subtlety, the Mitans expanded into depth. So which was the better? 'How can we know the dancer from the dance?'

But they both gave way to Tim's bottle. An '82 Latour, it was a wine which the Valkyries would have been proud to serve to the warriors on their saddlebags: a bottle worthy to have welcomed Labalaba on his arrival in Valhalla. Ready now, but only just, it should still be at its peak in 2072, to celebrate 100 years since his implacable defiance and glorious fall. I have had one finer wine: the Latour '45. What a house, whose finest years are fully worthy of gods and heroes. The rest of us can forget unworthiness, in joy.

## ~ The charms of old Paris and the naughtiest girl of the 20th century ~

Paris used to be the most self-confident city in the world. Brash, assertive, boastful: Manhattan claimed to be the best. Cool, elegant, sophisticated, supercilious: Paris knew that it was the best. This is no longer true. Paris has lost its élan, and that has created a love–hate relationship with the UK. Everyone seems to know someone who is working in London. The ones left in Paris cannot decide whether to punish us or join us: to hope that Brexit fails — or to fear that Brexit might fail, and keep able young Frenchmen from job opportunities in London.

*Flics* everywhere, tattiness, tension: one is reluctant to acknowledge the successes of evil, but terrorism is at the core of Paris's problems. In this most civilised of cities, there is a fear that civilisation is losing control. On all sides, there is a loss of faith in the French system: economic, administrative and diplomatic. *La grande illusion* of post-war French foreign policy — Europe as a French jockey on a German horse — now seems just that: an illusion. One must always remember that French political self-belief has never been more than a sticking plaster to cover deep wounds: 1940, Vichy, the Liberation, which did not happen quite in the way that de Gaulle described. When the French fall off their high horse, they suffer.

Yet we must not exaggerate. In Paris, you are convinced that there is only one way to translate chic — Parisienne. The girls have an allure: a blend of gamine and grace, haute couture and mischief. That got us talking about the naughtiest girl of the 20th century, Pamela Harriman, a Dorset aristocrat who ended her life as the American ambassador to France, with so many adventures along the way. Few husbands could resist her; no wife ever trusted her. I once reviewed a biography of her, and one paragraph had the lawyers reaching for smelling salts. There was no use my protesting that all the facts were in the book. But death is the ultimate antidote to a libel writ, so here it is. 'She was the grandest of *grandes horizontales*, the most luxurious of *poules de luxe.* "I carry my house on my back," she often said. She certainly got all her houses on her back.' Apropos horizontal, she was probably the first horizontal collaborator of the war, but with an ally. Her role as Averell Harriman's mistress undoubtedly facilitated cooperation between the UK and the US. The unit of charm ought to be a milli-Helen: a face that would launch one ship. Pamela's collaboration may well have launched a number of lend-lease warships. Around that time, a young officer ran into her father, the then Lord Digby. As she was already ... well-known, he put his voice into neutral before asking after her. 'Pammy's doing very well. I was worried about her coming up to London, because she's used to a quiet life down here. But she's turned out to be a good manager. I don't give her much of an allowance and I can't imagine the War Office pays her much — but do you know: she's got a flat in Berkeley Square.'

We indulged in these reminiscences over wine made by one of the best female vignerons in France. Nathalie Tollot of Tollot-Beaut, herself a gamine enchantment, produces excellent Burgundies throughout the price range. The lesser wines, Bourgogne blanc or rouge, Savigny-lès-Beaune, Chorey-lès-Beaune, are always good value. But Jacques, our host, had a couple of special bottles: the Beaune-Grèves '88 and a Corton-Bressandes of the same vintage. An expert, he was well aware that 1988 Burgundies are contentious. There are those who claim that they are over the hill, and those who insist that they will never climb it. We awaited with expectation. The Grèves was past its best, but only a little. It would have been better three years ago, and now needs drinking. But the Bressandes was outstanding. Fully exposed, certainly, but its silkiness was still reinforced by power. If only that were true of France.

## ~ Burgundies that taste of T.S. Eliot ~

Eliot. After 50 years of trying to make sense of his verse, and at the risk of admitting to rampant philistinism, I propose three conclusions. At his best, he is one of the finest poets in the language. Partly because he is straining language and thought to the uttermost — an analogy with the final Beethoven piano sonatas — he is sometimes incomprehensible: sometimes, indeed, falls into arrant pseudery. Finally, his anti-Semitism before the war, his rejection of *Animal Farm* after it: this great man and devout Christian was not exempt from original sin.

'Gerontion'. 'The Jew squats on the window sill … spawned in some estaminet of Antwerp …' We turn our eye from the page in revulsion and pity. Even before Auschwitz, how could one of the finest sensibilities of our era have written that? A few lines later: 'After such knowledge, what forgiveness?' Truly, this was a man of sorrows and acquainted with grief. Much can be forgiven to such a tortured soul.

England. Eliot may have moved to England and embraced Englishness: 'History is now and England.' But he could never immerse himself in the clod-hopping stolidity of the England deep-down things: the pint of beer in the country pub, the discreet cleverness of an Englishman who pretends to be anti-intellectual and turns out to have read a lot of books — the 'Dearly Beloved' in church on Sunday. In England at its best and wisest, there is a eupeptic stoicism, an understanding that life is far too important to be taken seriously. Poor Eliot: he could never escape for long from seriousness.

'Macavity'. All that said, there are the cat poems. Necessary light relief after you have been trying to fight your way across *The Waste Land*, they must also have been light relief for him: his version of Dearly Beloved. 'In my beginning is my end.' I started to read Eliot as a pretentious schoolboy who thought that it would be easy to understand the human condition. Half a century later, in sight, I suppose, of 'In my end is my beginning,' it is more a matter of 'These fragments I have stored against my ruins.' But I shall grapple with Eliot as long as my wits endure.

'Voluptuary sweetness.' Those thoughts, welcome, self-indulgent, unwelcome, forced themselves upon me after a tasting of white 2015s from Bernard Vallet and the house of Pierre Bourré. In 2015, the sun burst forth over Burgundy with its benefactions. The result was a Ceres, a Proserpine of a hugely ripe vintage, like a voluptuous girl painted by Titian or Rubens, with the obvious risk of blowsiness. But there is an advantage. The lesser wines are ready for early drinking. Thus it was with Bernard's bottles.

'Midwinter spring is its own season.' On a filthy evening in February, while one might be fighting down envy of better-organised friends who always evade the final phase of winter by decamping to the Caribbean, Bernard's Auxey-Duresses and Pernand-Vergelesses were wonderfully restorative. Happy in their own skin, these are village wines with no pretensions to a higher status. Yet they have the promise and the charm of a gentler season: an almost Apollonian serenity. Winter shall have no dominion. These are the harbingers of summer.

Other village wines can aspire further. Bernard's Meursault was thoroughly sound, his Puligny-Montrachet as good as many a Premier Cru. At that level, the palm went to another Meursault, a Premier Cru Les Perrières, absolutely not a wine for early drinking. As to how long the '15s will last, everything will depend on the grower. We should not underestimate the alchemical power of the best Burgundians. In two millennia, their ability to blend the heat of the sun and the minerality of the terroir has not failed them. Their right arms have not lost their cunning.

## ~ From kittens to claret:
## an ideal education ~

Call me a sentimental old whatever, but watching a four-year-old hearing *The Tale of Samuel Whiskers* for the first time, read by someone who could do the police in different voices, took one as far from the Waste Land as is possible. It also made me think about moggies, which brought back memories of a trip to Kabul. Outside the Portakabin where we were billeted, there was a notice: 'Please do not bring cats into the living quarters.' No one puts up an instruction like that without the expectation that it will be disobeyed. One can imagine why, and how very British. It is to the credit of the brutal and licentious, living in cramped conditions, exposed to constant danger, that they had sentimentality left for local felines.

A few of those were prowling near the entrance to the cabins. Although they did not look starving, they were not overnourished. But I am sure that they often benefited from military generosity. Camp Bastion would be a good posting for an Afghan cat. Anyway, we were eating our evening meal, which included a curious piece of sausage-type meat, of a reddish colour. Was it animal, vegetable or mineral? Perhaps we were being offered renditioned carcase broiled on depleted uranium. I chucked mine in the direction of a cat. After sniffing the offering as intently as an oenophile assessing a newly poured wine, the animal put its nose in the air and stalked off, with the air of a Belgravia Siamese rejecting inferior smoked salmon. The sausage was clearly corked. To a chorus of 'If even that cat …', most of my colleagues immediately discarded theirs.

I should have brought the sausage back for Professor Branestawm to analyse. This is a scientific friend of mine, who is also the most distinguished male feminist in these islands since John Stuart Mill. He has six daughters, who were each given a kitten. There was a rule: cats did not spend the night in the house. Feline cunning added to feminine wiles: one can imagine how strictly that rule was obeyed. The cats have taken after Moppet and Mittens rather than that wimp Tom Kitten. All good mousers and ratters, they relish hunting rabbits and have seen off foxes.

The girls' education did not consist only of fluff and fur. Their father insisted that, at least until O-Level, the core curriculum should include Latin, physics and maths. But there was little need to keep them up to the mark. Academically, they thrive, as in other respects. In the interests of diversity and the environment, the Professor decreed that the girls must learn to shoot. All have, proficiently. In every respect, this household triumphantly refutes the claim that the number of daughters a man has is in proportion to his wickedness in a previous life.

After such a contribution to equality, a chap is entitled to a decent glass of wine. The other evening, he produced a '95 Léoville Barton. Mature, harmonious as the Pastoral in the hands of a great symphony orchestra, it would surely be hard to surpass. But a '97 Margaux succeeded. As so often, the 1855 classification was vindicated. The first growth was an even higher peak. I have always insisted that whereas you drink a Pauillac, you undress a Margaux. This wine justified that dictum. It had femininity, structure, subtlety and power. It proves a point which the Professor's daughters can take for granted. A girl can succeed in a man's world.

But there may be an exception. In Bordeaux, the house of Latour still towers over the landscape, that most masculine of clarets. Although it is not always the greatest wine of the year, it does win the blue riband more often than not. We finished with a '99, the highest peak, still shrouded in mist. Grandeur awaits, but that wine needs several years. If they are good girls — or perhaps even if they are naughty ones — the Professor's daughters might be drinking that wine in decades to come.

## ~ Bloody Marys and the funniest woman in the House of Lords ~

To the Western Isles, or at least to its embassy in Belgravia. Boisdale restaurant always claims to be extra-territorial. There was an awards ceremony, and the principal recipient was a remarkable old girl. Ninety-four years into an extraordinarily diverse life, Jean Trumpington is one of the funniest people I have ever met. She is also one of the bravest. She was born in easy circumstances, a child of the affluent upper middle classes, and the first disruption occurred when her mother lost a lot of money in the Great Crash. Her family did not exactly become poor, but she had her first lesson in adversity, and on the unwisdom of taking anything for granted.

At the beginning of the war, she set off to be a land-girl on David Lloyd George's farm. She is now the sole survivor of the various females whom the old goat chased around his fields. Then came codebreaking at Bletchley Park. Jean had the right attitude to the war. When on duty, hard work in the national interest; when off duty, hard play in the interests of fun. Air raids merely spiced up the merriment. Under wartime restrictions, restaurants were not allowed to charge more than five bob for dinner. That made the Ritz a bargain. Jean enjoyed herself.

After the war, she escaped Attlee's austerity by moving to New York: a lot more fun. She returned to England with a husband, Alan Barker, one of the foremost schoolmasters of his generation. By the time he was 50, he was a headmaster, apparently assured of all the glories that beak-dom could offer. It seemed inevitable that he would become a chairman of various public bodies, a lauded recipient of honours and emoluments.

That was not to be. A terrible stroke left him disabled. During what should have been his highest-earning years, he was an invalid needing expensive care. But a girl who had fended off Lloyd George and helped to defeat the Nazis was not to be deterred. Out of suffering came stoicism and fightback. Jean had been involved in local politics. She now intensified her commitment, came to Margaret Thatcher's attention, and was sent to the House of Lords. There was a problem. What was she to call herself? Baroness Barker: no. Peers who do not wish to use their surnames often take their title from their home base. She lived in Six Mile Bottom. Doubly no. She settled on Trumpington, which is so appropriate. The word reverberates like a Handelian drum roll in a quick march.

She and Their Lordships' House revelled in one another. At the end of term before a recess, the Tory whips' office holds an impromptu drinks party: more of a drink-up party. Bloody Marys with Clamato often feature. Jean was sitting on a banquette, under which were more tins of Clamato. One of the younger whips said, 'Jean, can I just come between your legs and ...' She interrupted. 'Any time, ducky.' A foolish and humourless girl who ran a colour supplement once almost redeemed herself by her choice of lunch guests: Jean and Nick Soames. Nick was praising the virtues of Virginia Bottomley, who is indeed as toothsome a wench as ever served in a cabinet. 'She fits in so well that we think of her as one of the chaps.' Silly girl: 'But she's a woman.' Soames: 'Of course she is. She's also one of the chaps.' S.G.: 'If you call a woman one of the chaps, you must be sick.' Jean, after removing the fag and the gin glass from her mouth: 'BALLS.'

To salute this great lady we drank wines supplied by the Rothschilds. Recently, they bought Château Rieussec, famous for sweet wines. They have produced a dry 'R' de Rieussec. Crisp, tart, subtle, sophisticated, it was excellent with shellfish. Near Limoux, they are producing Domaine de Baronarques, a blend of Bordeaux varietals and southern grapes: grenache, malbec, syrah. We tasted the '03, '07 and '13. These are serious bottles, fully worthy of a toast: 'Long live Trumps.'

'The Au pair who mixed a case of,
2013 petrus pomerol from the cellar, into the
glühwein instead of the 'special offer' of
12 for the price of 6 from 'The Wine Bazaar !'

# ~ The only good thing about the
# Soviet Union was cheap caviar ~

I know an immensely grand aristocratic lady, impeccably mannered, with a regal grace and presence, who cannot be trusted near a tin of caviar. Apart from scoffing far more than her share, she will eventually make off with the tin itself, to lick it clean. Those of us from lesser social milieux should not only treat this as a lesson in etiquette. There are sound environmental arguments for her behaviour. Caviar is so precious, so rare, that it is an ecological crime to waste a single egg. When her ladyship is on the prowl, there is no danger of that.

Such thoughts came to me over the weekend, while musing on large themes over a small tin. It brought back memories and also made one think about the unforeseen consequences of political change. In the early 1990s, I sometimes travelled to eastern Europe with Julian Amery, a wonderful mentor. Largely because he was born in the wrong era, Julian was unlucky in his British political career. But in the crumbling Soviet empire, he was treated as a figure of the first importance. Everyone assumed that he had been foreign secretary, at least. In terms of entertainment, he always had two requests: gypsy music and caviar. I was keener on the caviar. But there was charm in hearing a useful fiddler accompanying an overflowing contralto, as Julian's face became wistful, his memories drawn back to his piratical wartime youth in the Balkans, when the surroundings would have been less plush, the music, if any, more intense, and little chance of caviar.

Around the end of the Soviet era, the place for caviar was Moscow. You went to a restaurant and were immediately identified as a dollar customer. You were escorted past a school dining hall full of Russians on benches, supervised by surly waitresses, being fed meatballs and watery spuds along with watery vodka. The balls contained God knows what.

Given that we foreigners were next door, one hoped that it was only depleted *meat*, and would not register on a Geiger counter.

We hard-currency payers dined on chairs, at tables: about the same level of comfort as the best restaurant in Blackpool during a party conference. The waitresses were better-looking than their Blackpool equivalents, and they were happy to ingratiate themselves in the hope of tips (no Blackpool waitress could have come within six letters of spelling 'ingratiate'). The prettier Muscovites might well be available for afters. As for the food, Blackpool could have done better — except for the caviar. That kept on coming, with decent vodka: why eat anything else, when it was so cheap?

You could also buy caviar in street markets: bring your own receptacle — receptacles were scarce — and fill it with dollops from a vat. One would have thought that there ought to have been outbreaks of food poisoning. I never heard of any. Equally, one would have assumed that there should be an international price for caviar. That was beyond Soviet organisational skills.

The Soviet Union is gone, and should be unlamented, even in Jeremy Corbyn's office. But I cannot help a certain nostalgia for the era of abundant caviar. Equally, the common agricultural policy is deplorable, but think of Tante Marie's chèvre and Oncle Bernard's saucisson: the boudin noir, the worn-out nags waiting to be entered for the knackers' stakes; all the other delights of a street market in Provence. Of all the trillions wasted in unnecessary government expenditure, subsidies to French artisanal farming are surely among the least deplorable.

Apropos France, we drank Grey Goose vodka with the caviar. That is a spirit to be sipped and savoured. Only an idiot would down it at a gulp. Indeed, it almost refutes George W. Bush's claim that France is an entrepreneur-free zone. Caviar, good vodka: there is no more ambrosial combination. It even made us feel relaxed about Donald Trump.

# ~ What wine is worthy of white truffle?
# It took us a few tries to be sure ~

A few days ago, on the Dorset/Somerset marches, autumn was still in orderly retreat. Although a pear tree's leaves had turned sere and yellow, the last fruit was still peeping through. Across the lawn, a horse chestnut was undressing, festooning the lawn with bronze. Out of a cloudless sky, a mild seasonal sun blessed the scene with a gentle glow, as if it were pouring Sauternes. Along the Ladies' Walk, the yellows and greens were reinforced by bushes in russet mantles and by the triumphant redness of acers and liquidambar. We could have almost been in the New England fall, at least for a few yards.

Autumn, fall: the two have profound resonances from different histories. As one might expect from its French name, autumn is full of good eating. This does not always take forms which the French would recognise, for it includes Brussels sprouts. Curious as it may seem, my friend Eyzie has an elective affinity with that vegetable. She is the Brillat-Savarin of the sprout. More generally, autumn is redolent of full barns, of well-stocked log sheds, of well-fattened pigs scoffing the last windfalls, heedless of their doom. Slaughtering day approaches. With the defences against winter well-prepared, wise households can approach the great feast of Christmas in a complacent spirit.

There would have been little of that in nascent New England. The fall of man: the fall of the year. It may be that the embattled colonists had lost the easy English assumption that spring would return. Across the Atlantic, the fall meant an impending exposure to the furious winter's rages. Splendid red trees, certainly, but how many red men were lurking among them? Admittedly the Puritans arrived with a harsh religion, but at least in the first era, there would have been nothing to mitigate the bleakness. If those early Americans had been minded to gloss over original sin, there would have been plenty to remind them of it.

In Dorset, religion has a much more Rosicrucian hue. If counties have a patron sin, Dorset's is gluttony. My friend Ro, a redoubtable forager, returned with a cornucopia of fungi: pied du mouton, chanterelles, orange birch boletes, cepes and parasols. What followed was transcendent simplicity, as he transformed them into bruschetta. Cook the fungi in oil, rub the toasted country bread with garlic, pile on the riches, add a further drizzle of oil — eat to repletion and reach for superlatives. Yet that was only the approach to the summit. Our next meal was based on an early season white truffle. There is only one way to describe such sensations. Imagine what Hillary Clinton must be feeling now, move 180 degrees opposite, double that, redouble it — and you are within hailing distance.

Yet Hillary had her revenge. To accompany fungi and tubers, we decided against cabernet sauvignon. Although Left-Bank claret works for almost everything except shellfish, it is not quite right for mushrooms. Chateauneuf du Pape Clos des Papes '02 should have been ideal, but the first two bottles we opened were pure vinegar: Château Clinton 2016. So we fell back on a Malescot St Exupéry 2000: a thoroughly acceptable line of retreat. For the truffle, returning to the original strategy (as opposed to the original sin) with trepidation, we tried a Bourgueil '76. Would it have lasted 40 years? There was an initial and deeply unpromising mustiness. It then began to open out in the glass, without achieving harmony. But after five minutes — could it have smelt the truffle? — it awakened to deliciousness.

So it is time to make an early New Year resolution; one I have made before, but always broken. Drink more Loire reds. There is lots of interest — including anything made by Jacky Blot — even if it will rarely match that Bourgueil, and even if one will rarely drink it with truffle.

# ~ Should NATO have embraced Russia? ~

An aeon ago, when I was first invited to the odd City lunch, there was a standard formula: G&T, white, red, port, brandy, cigars, with stumps drawn at around a Test match tea interval. But there was a problem. By 8 a.m. local time, when Manhattan was champing at the telephone, London would be at lunch. By the time the call was returned, it would be apparent that lunching had taken place. 'My Dear Cyrus, how nice to hear your voice. Are you planning to cross the big pond? If so, we'll have a jolly good lunch.' Cyrus thought to himself: 'Is that all those Limeys ever do: have lunch?' Within a few years, post-Big Bang, the Cyruses did cross the big pond, but not to enjoy lunch. There is an assumption, reinforced by priggishness, that the ensuing puritanism has improved the City. Is that necessarily so?

Anyway, there is at least one building where the old rites are still used. Last week, I went to an immensely stimulating luncheon. We drank Corton-Charlemagne, Dme-Bonneau du Martray, '09, followed by a L'Évangile '01. It was a tribute to the quality of the talk that we did not spend more time analysing and praising those superb wines. Our host had assembled a lively table. There were formidable bankers and lawyers, the historian Michael Burleigh and a few former diplomats: some from the official wing of the FCO, others from its transpontine branch.

A couple of Enigma machines were on display, which was appropriate, for we were discussing Russia. I was sufficiently temerarious to argue that the West could have done more to embrace post-Soviet Russia. Once we had won the Cold War, we should have scrapped our concepts while retaining our weapons systems. We needed a new system of collective security, one capable of including the new Russia.

NATO had been established to keep the Germans down, the Russians out and the Americans in. The first of those objectives is long since obsolete. After the liberation of East Germany, Poland, Czechoslovakia, Hungary et al., the second was surely less pressing. As for the third, we still needed NATO, if only to ensure a continuing American presence: the Europeans would never have been prepared to spend enough to defend themselves. But with the end of the Soviet Union, the West had no reason for a strategic quarrel with the Russians. It should not have been impossible to create structures which reflected this. Instead, we encouraged NATO expansion, in a haphazard way. One can understand why the Baltic states wanted to join. But admitting them merely undermined NATO's credibility. De Gaulle said that the Americans would never have swapped Detroit for Düsseldorf. Fortunately, we never found out whether he was right. But no one is going to swap one of their cities for Riga. It would be fatuous to pretend otherwise.

Although it is also easy to see why Ukraine and Georgia want to join NATO, that cannot happen. Those countries are condemned to live in a dangerous neighbourhood, and fantasies are useless. If your dwelling is next to a fierce bear's cave, the odd pot of propitiatory honey might help. There is no point in shouting rude slogans in the hope that your big brother will rush to the rescue. Big brother is good for a resolution at the UN, nothing more — and anyway, the bear will veto it.

Others, much more expert than I, doubted whether it would ever have been possible to reach an accommodation with Russia. Though the subject was too complex for consensus, there were two points of agreement. First, the Cold War had restarted; second, the next ten years were going to be a fascinating period, but not necessarily a successful one. The Évangile, as intellectually rigorous as any Graves, was the perfect counterpoint to our session. It engendered a wholly appropriate mood of eupeptic pessimism.

# ~ With great wine comes great anxiety ~

We were surpassing Sydney Smith. His idea of heaven was pâté de foie gras to the sound of trumpets. Our version was an un pâtéd foie: even more delicious. Though no one had laid on Jeremiah Clarke, there was music: a bottle of Doisy Daëne '75. In most of the Bordeaux area, 1975 was an austere year, and the fear was that the wines would live and die as sleeping beauties. Well, the Dozy Dean had awakened, to a harmony of structure and sweetness. There seems only one sensible response to such pleasures: 'God's in his heaven and all's right with the world.'

Instead, however, the conversation took a melancholy tone. We started with that unendingly paradoxical figure, W.B. Yeats. In the Hammersmith of the 1890s, old women of both senses often met to talk nonsense. Phrenology, ouija boards, séances: these suburban Owen Glendowers tried to call spirits from the vasty deep, and were lucky that no one called for the men in white coats. But no such gathering, however absurd, was complete until Yeats had joined it. Nor was he ever fully cured, as some of his later mystical effusions testify. Much of it is reminiscent of that most undozy — and tragic — of deans, Jonathan Swift, as he descended into lunacy. 'Why do they call him Aristophanes? Because he had such airy stoff an he's head.' So, often, did Yeats.

Yet he was also one of the major political intelligences of all time. 'Easter, 1916': has there ever been a more profound political poem? Then there is the definitive four-word history of Ireland, and of Israel/Palestine: 'Great hatred, little room.' Or what about that call to arms which should inspire anyone of a Conservative disposition: 'The fascination of what's difficult'? But it is followed by an instant and salutary corrective: '... Has dried the sap out of my veins, and rent / Spontaneous joy and natural content / Out of my heart.' To think of that in the presence of foie gras and

Barsac? An even greater student of the human condition than Yeats has the explanation: 'Lord, what fools these mortals be.'

We compounded our folly by moving on to the indispensable cliché. No phrase ever becomes a cliché unless it was originally redolent of salt, pith and wisdom. Then it grows mouldy and has to be set aside, at least for a generation. In the 1890s, 'he has the defects of his qualities' was so grossly overused that it would surely have provoked a groan — to such an extent that it was forgotten. Now, it is restored to pristine wit, at least for a season. But one cliché cannot be discarded. 'Things fall apart, the centre cannot hold ... the best lack all conviction, the worst are full of passionate intensity.' Thus is summarised the course of world events since 1914. Thus did Yeats toll the funeral bell of the Enlightenment.

On reflection, that might explain the absurdities of Hammersmith, and the mysticism. Nietzsche had warned that if you stared into the abyss for too long, it will stare back at you. He did; it did. Perhaps Yeats was trying to avoid a similar fate and knew that no rescue was to be found in reason.

On a dark winter night, small children will often tell each other ghost stories, so successfully that they are terrified to be left in their bedrooms, more than ever convinced that there are bears under the bed. We were rescued from the adult equivalent by some Viña Tondonia Gran Reserva '04, which I highly commend, not that there is ever a disappointment from that noble producer. This is a *gaudeamus igitur* of a wine. Eat, drink and be merry — and ignore the next line.

# ~ The no-nonsense greatness of Australian wine ~

Any Australian who admits to not having convict ancestors loses caste. When granted a coat of arms, the smart ones always include fetters. It is the Oz equivalent of claiming that your ancestors came over with William the Conqueror. But it was not always thus. In the Adelaide of the 1890s, there was a family called Strangeways Wigley, who had paid for their tickets and never stopped swanking about it. But they had a blot on the escutcheon in the form of young Robert. He was determined to rectify the lack of criminal blood.

In those days, a pieman — as opposed to a swagman — used to sell his wares in the town centre. He was especially popular towards the end of the evening, when the ockers needed ballast to soak up the grog. But one night, Robert hitched his horse to the pieman's wagon and took off. A glorious chase ensued. The entire town took part. The air was full of view-hallooing; all the men were waving their corked hats. Finally, Robert was captured and spent the night in the lock-up. The locals were delighted that the snobs had been discomfited. The Strangeways Wigleys were mortified. Before he could add to the disgrace, Robert was transported, to the wine country in McLaren Vale.

There, he planted the Wirra Wirra vineyards. But the course of true winemaking never did run smooth. Although he was a good taster, the other aspects of the trade were neglected. The bush reasserted itself. Rescue came in 1969 from the late Gregory Trotter. Trotty — the customary usage — was not a snob. He may well have been the swagman's descendant. But he created a serious vinery, with a range of impressive bottles, too few of which find their way to the UK.

There is a difference between the Californian and Australian wine trades. When they describe their wares, some Californians sound like ballet teachers. There is none of that among the penal colonists. Their word for precious is 'Pommy poofter'. Trotty brought science and expertise to the business, but would never have admitted it. If anyone had accused him of an Etonian horror of being caught working, it would be amusing to decide who would have been more horrified: Trotty, or Eton.

When he flew to Melbourne, he could not be dissuaded but always wore the same costume: shorts and welly-boots. Perhaps he overestimated the chances of *rus in urbe* in that city, and hoped to come upon an unsuspecting sheep, safely grazing. He decided to call one of his wines Angelus because he liked the name. Château Angelus, a premier grand cru from St Emilion, was unamused. A formidable-looking letter arrived at Wirra Wirra. As it was in French, Trotty and his wellies had to set off to the city to find a translator. The Australians were instructed to cease and desist, or face *peine forte et dure*. So the name was changed to Dead Ringer.

We tasted the '09 the other evening. The name is an exaggeration. For a start, Angelus has hardly any cabernet sauvignon; Dead Ringer, 100 per cent. But it was jolly good. Drinking well now, it will last for at least a decade. At around a tenth of the price of its French elder brother, it is excellent value. So were the Absconder, a grenache; the 12th Man chardonnay — and the Church Block, a Shiraz, merlot and cab. sauv. blend. All of them were young and forward; none is likely to fall apart any time soon. We were dining in a London neighbourhood which supplied many involuntary colonists; Bethnal Green, at the Water House Project, a dining club cum restaurant which I would highly recommend. Committed to their art, its foodie owners are delighted to discuss menus and ingredients. Our food ranged from really good dinner-party nosh to a couple of dishes worth a Michelin rosette. Wirra Wirra in Bethnal Green; I suppose that is called diversity.

## ~ Wine, women and willow: a perfect combo for a perfect English summer day ~

The first time I went to Lord's was in 1970, just before the unofficial Test series which replaced the cancelled South African one. I was in the Long Room, discussing Barry Richards, one of the most elegant batsmen of all time. He did not seem to hit the ball. It was as if he had caressed it, after which it would rocket to the boundary. Has there ever been an opener whose stroke-play gave such aesthetic pleasure?

An incredibly old buffer joined in our conversation: 'I always knew young Richards would be good. Came over here as a 16-year-old schoolboy and hit a six off me.' Who was this pompous so-and-so? Someone of a similar vintage promptly clapped him on the shoulder: 'Morning, Alec.' Er, yes: when Barry Richards was 16, Alec Bedser would have been 43. He would still not have been giving away sixes.

Cricket is the greatest sporting spectacle. Before the current Test series began, two conclusions were being drawn. First, that the Indians would win easily. Second, that Test cricket was under threat from various ersatz versions, mostly sponsored by bookmakers from the subcontinent. Now it is not only political commentators who seem incapable of predicting the past, let alone the future.

After a riveting first Test, the Indians were unlucky at Lord's. It always seemed likely that the side which won the toss would win the match. The conditions encouraged a magnificent display of English swing-bowling. In response, the Indians' technique collapsed and possibly also their morale. For a couple of sessions, we seemed to be back several decades, in the era when India would be captained by some stately Maharajah, and their batsmen would be retreating towards the square-leg umpire before the English quick had started his run-up. The Indians now face a challenge of character. If they can surmount it, this series will still have its opportunities.

Cricket: the gentlest game, the most beautiful game, the hardest game. Once, on a village green, pint in hand, my eye fell on a strange-looking individual in a dog collar. Both burly and shrunken, he looked like a Wodehousian curate with a ravaged soul. I tried that paradox on my neighbour, who told me that I spoke truer than I knew. The chap was indeed a curate, and had been a mighty if unsophisticated smiter of a cricket ball. Once, properly middled, it had soared over the boundary. And landed on a baby's head. Death was instantaneous, for the baby. In the clergyman's case, life had become a living death. Everyone told him that it was not his fault. The infant's parents had forgiven him. He could not forgive himself. God. Around me was sunshine and laughter and cries of 'same again'. Except on that poor fellow's face; it bore the stigmata of Hellish suffering.

Cricket goes with wine. Arlott, Gower, Botham are only three examples among many. Jacques Kallis — is he the greatest South African cricketer since Barry Richards? — is now running a vineyard. On Friday, at Lord's but in the Middlesex hospitality area, we were lucky to meet Laura Angus, a delightful Australian girl. As was often said about the Waugh brothers, what a pity that her ancestors were transported. We drank an excellent sauvignon blanc from Marlborough (New Zealand), a South African pinotage and a great deal of beer. Laughter, stories, glasses constantly recharged and an England win almost inevitable, weather permitting. What a splendid day.

# ~ Adventures of a hell-cat in heaven ~

Over the weekend I officiated at a funeral. Earlier in the morning there had been lowering rain clouds, but by the time we dug the grave there were blue skies to salute Albert's passing. He deserved them. It was also appropriate that he died just before the anniversary of Jutland, for this was a feline dreadnought. Black as the darkest night and a prodigious slaughterer of vermin, he also ranged well beyond his owners' policies in search of tabby cats on heat or toms up for a fight. No one knew exactly how old he was. He had arrived 20 years ago as a young stray, to a family who was not sure whether they liked cats — always an irresistible challenge to any self-respecting moggy — and set about earning his keep by massacring rats and mice.

There were regular bewailings over the inevitable songbirds; Albert was un-bellable. Nor was he an effusively affectionate cat. When he sat on a lap there was always an air of condescension. In his last years he would often park himself on the husband's chaotic desk, in the midst of a chaotic study. This was popular. Albert had a knack of reclining on a pile of letters from Her Majesty's Revenue and Customs, which provided an excuse for delaying their opening. All in all, he had become part of the household.

Six years ago, the owners decided that it was time for him to take his sweater, at least in some respects. As far as they could tell — and the complaints from other owners seemed to bear this out — he was still winning his battles. But by then it was Borodino rather than Austerlitz. His earflaps were increasingly ragged: the scars increasingly angry. So he was gelded — with no discernible effect on his behaviour.

After we laid him to rest below the terrace on which he had often sunned himself, I delivered the eulogy. 'Well, old friend, so here it is at last, the distinguished thing. You may now be able to answer all the great questions. If so, the celestial authorities might not yet realise what has hit them. One can imagine the capellmeister of the Heavenly Host apologising to the Almighty. "Eternal Father, I am so sorry. I've never heard the music of the spheres sound as rough. But none of the Cherubims and the Seraphims could hit a note. They were complaining that some tomcat's yowlings had kept them awake all night: not enough sleep to last for the twinkling of an eye. Some of the younger ones are saying that he is obviously a hell-cat who should never have been allowed in here, for he will be as troublesome as a rebel angel." Then God would summon the mightiest warrior angel and the greatest warrior saint. "Michael, George: pray track down this new cat on the block and explain to him the concept of eternal peace."

'No doubt the powers above would devise a modus vivendi which did not involve deportation. Even so, if heaven is perfection, Albert, you have presumably been restored to your full Nimrodic grandeur, in which case cat lovers among the Blessed will shortly be competing for the attentions of some scampering black kittens.

'Or is all that just a charming fantasy, and you will be lying for ever in an earthen basket, among the surroundings which you revelled in? If so, it may not have been an eternal life, but it was a fulfilled one. You took pleasure; you gave pleasure. Well done, thou good and faithful moggy.'

We toasted his passing in a splendid champagne: Henri Giraud Hommage à François Hémart. Our hosts had just brought back a people-carrier load from Ay. As a relatively new fizz on the block, it is still good value. But its price is bound to rise. One or two girls thought that some should be poured as a libation, but opinion was against them. Anthropomorphism must have its limits. Even such a grand pussy cat does not deserve grand cru champagne.

'The Arriviste who added ice from the
bucket to his 1995 Böerl and Kroff
Champagne!'

# ~ On the trail of a Burgundian Holy Grail ~

It was a scene evoking the first movement of the Pastoral Symphony. The evening sunshine was caressing the verdant woods at the top of a hill. It was only a low hill; there seemed nothing especial about this sweet rural scene. But just below the woods, the upper slopes contain some of the most valuable agricultural land in the world, producing magnificent wine. We were looking up from Gevrey-Chambertin towards the domain of the grands crus.

Not everything was as joyous in recent years, Dijon has expanded. France, with the same population, is two and a half times as large as the UK, so land is cheap. There is nothing to discourage the shapeless sprawl that disfigures the surroundings of many US cities: garages, car showrooms and — worst of all — fast-food outlets.

There used to be a wonderful restaurant on the main road at Morey-St-Denis. Largely for lorry drivers, it was run by a splendid couple. At lunchtime, in order to entice customers, Madame, a lady of a certain age, would parade outside in all weathers, in a plunging neckline and a skirt so short that the vulgar might have called it a manhole cover. Indoors, there was a fug of smoke, plus excellent food at €9 for three courses. The main one would often be a boeuf bourguignon, rich and unctuous, just like grandmère would have made. There was no choice of final dish: merely generous access to a cheeseboard that would have graced a multi-rosetted restaurant. Plentiful, satisfying and cheap, the wine came in unlabelled bottles, usually the declassified product of a serious vineyard, no doubt bought at mates' rates. The breathalyser had not yet impinged on the camionneurs' consciousness. God knows how the place made a profit, but I am sure that it sold nothing but food. Although le patron was endlessly genial, he was built like a prop forward. Anyway, and alas, the place is no more, while Kentucky Fried Chicken atrocities proliferate.

But the best parts of Burgundy are unchanging. Many vineyards have cellars like the crypts of Romanesque churches, with masonry that looks as if ancient stones had been reused. The ceilings are blackened, by yeast from the wine and by the breath of oenophiles over the centuries, plus the webs of long-dead spiders. Quite often there are no spittoons. You spit on the gravel beneath the racks of barrels.

The crypt-like appearance is appropriate. Winemaking has a sacramental quality. To produce it, the vignerons are consecrating the blood of the soil, in pursuit of a Burgundian Holy Grail. This is why wine cellars are glorious places that always inspire good talk. The stories circulated with the glasses. An elderly wine merchant was advising a new recruit: 'Remember, lad, a glimpse at the label is worth 20 years in the trade.' There are two rich and successful Yorkshire businessmen, considerable oenophiles with cellars to match, who still talk broad Yorkshire because they would hate anyone to think they had grown soft and southern. It also helps to intimidate London bankers. On wine, they are endlessly rivalrous and try never to agree about anything. In a recent argument, one said to the other: 'You can't be a label fucker all your life.'

The rest of us had come to Burgundy in a trip organised by Richard Berkley-Matthews of Clarion Wines to address a vital intellectual question. There has been a general assumption that 2015 will be a great vintage. This led a lot of buyers to overlook the '14s. There is no question that the '15s are full of fruit and power. But some of us concluded that the 2014s might be even better. They had subtlety, minerality and, above all, harmony between acid and fruit, like a mailed fist in a silken glove.

In the next column, I shall go into detail about the bottles and the vignerons. For the interim, amateurs of Burgundy should think 2014.

# ~ A thirst for justice: the wit and wisdom of Oliver Wendell Holmes ~

Justice Oliver Wendell Holmes, a great common lawyer, was an adornment to the American Supreme Court. His wisdom is still cited in common-law jurisdictions throughout the world. Any English lawyer who would prefer to exchange Holmes's incisive rulings — which usually amount to common sense elevated to a Platonic idea — for some European mush based on supposed human rights, reveals himself as a legal numbskull who so hates his own country that he cannot bear its successes, not least of which is the principle of freedom under the rule of law.

Holmes's long life was a chronicle of American evolution. He would have been entitled to call his memoirs 'The history of the United States in my own times'. At the beginning of the Civil War he joined the Union army. Shortly afterwards, as a young officer, he was stationed on the northern bank of the Potomac helping to man the ramparts. A tall man appeared, insouciant of Confederate snipers across the river. 'Keep down, you fool,' cried Holmes. The long fellow did, and as he passed said: 'Thank you, Lieutenant.' It was President Lincoln.

About 70 years later, another president came across Holmes reading Plato's *Republic* in the original. 'Why are you reading Plato in Greek, Justice Holmes?' enquired Franklin Roosevelt. 'To improve my mind, Mr President.'

Holmes's legal aphorisms were equally pithy. It was he who declared, in a debate about freedom of speech, that no one was entitled to shout 'fire' in a crowded theatre. He also stated that a man was entitled to swing his arm with its fist as vigorously as he chose, as long as it did not come into contact with another man's nose.

But I was citing the formidable Judge in a wholly un-legal context. When he was about 90, and conversing with another ancient Justice —

let us call him Smith — a girl law clerk sashayed past, with a double ration of the Platonic idea of youthful glory: a lovely face and a pert bottom. 'Ah, Smith,' nostalgised Holmes, 'to be 70 again.'

A group of us, still young enough to dread the onset of 70, still on the 'anec' side of dotage, were sitting around a dining table, finishing some good bottles with port to come, and remembering the dinner parties — or more accurately scoffing evenings — of our youth; around a kitchen table, over a great vat of spag bol and a large supply of plonk. In those days, everyone brought at least one bottle, none of which had any pretension to quality, all of which were drunk.

As years passed and we all moved beyond student mores, questions of wine etiquette arose. Some felt able to buy wine not for immediate consumption, to offer more sophisticated menus and to construct a wine strategy which did not depend on the arrival of armfuls of cheerful litres. There would be occasional cultural clashes. A less advanced friend would proffer a bottle and be miffed when it was not opened. He may have assumed that the host was snaffling it for private consumption, when the host actually regarded it as barely casserole quality.

A lot of reminiscences followed. In the early eighties, supermarkets were full of 'Bulgarian' cabernet sauvignon, good value at a quaffing price. A number of my friends adopted it as their table wine. Then supplies dried up. It may be that the Cape vineyards had found other outlets — or perhaps the Bulgarians had become fed up with marketing South African wine as theirs. But even at that time, most of us were moving from quantity to quality, along the primrose paths of dalliance from *vin ordinaire* to *grand cru classe*. Everyone had a story about the transformative power of a great bottle. Mine concerned the deputy editor of *The Spectator*, now a blissful new mother — unto us, a son is born. I recall her delight in a bottle of '88 Calon-Ségur. We ought to find her something similar, to fortify the milk.

# ~ Wine merchants might just be the happiest people in the world ~

A delightful girl came to see me this morning. She is helping with the research for a biography of David Cameron. Someone had told her that he was not comfortable in his own skin. There was only one reply to that: balls. I have never known anyone so much at ease with himself.

That discussion made me consider the concept of *bien dans sa peau*. There was Cardus's marvellous description of Emmott Robinson: 'It was as if God had taken a piece of strong Yorkshire clay, moulded it into human form, breathed life into it and said: "Thy name is Emmott Robinson and tha shall open t' bowling from Pavilion End."' That was clearly a happy man, as long as Yorkshire were winning.

But I decided that the drink trade breeds a more durable contentment, not dependent on the vagaries of the wicket or the umpires. I considered friends and acquaintances who have devoted their working lives to selling beverages: Richard Berkley-Matthews, Hew Blair, Ronnie Cox, Cassidy Dart, Andrew Sheepshanks, Andrew Smith, Mark Walford. In every case, their career was a vocation. Like Emmott Robinson, they had been put on earth to do what they wanted to do. 'I often wonder what the vintners buy / One half as precious as the stuff they sell.'

There is now another name to add to the list. Four years ago, Jasper Morris produced a book, *Inside Burgundy*, which lives up to its title. As Steven Spurrier writes in the introduction, it has been 'written by someone who has and does walk the land: you can stand with him, look to your left, spot the dip that was a quarry, note how the slope turns just here towards the morning sun'. But this is not just a peasant's-eye Burgundy. It is a distillation of history, literature and oenology. Jasper has read everything written on the subject and distilled it in lucid prose. He has not only mastered the literature; he has produced a work of literature, one of the finest wine books ever written.

Jasper has also worked his palate hard for several decades. The reader benefits from a profound experience of tasting. Indeed, our author offers his own reclassification of every important Burgundy. There are some promotions, but quite a few Cortons are knocked down from grand to premier cru. How should an oenophile choose between Jasper's book and Clive Coates's one, mentioned here a few weeks ago? That is easy. He would want them both, and it would be fascinating to compare their verdicts.

At a recent lunch, we drew on Jasper. The theme was Burgundies from 1993. In his overall assessment of that year, Jasper refers to troublesome weather leading to a difficult growing season and awkward tannins. His conclusion: some potentially long-lived wines, but 'it is never going to be a graceful vintage'.

Our first wine came close to refuting him. A Meursault Les Luchets, Domaine Roulot, was superb. It is only a village wine, and as such would have reason to show its age, but this was classic Meursault: almost up to grand cru standard. We moved on to a Clos Saint-Jacques, Domaine Armand Rousseau. It would probably have been classified as a grand cru but for the disdainful behaviour of a previous proprietor, and Jasper rates it on the borderline between premier and grand. Its owner had drunk a bottle over the weekend and found it superb. He provided two more, and they could not have been more different. The first had a marvellous nose but refused to open out. When it finally did so, opinion was divided. I thought that it was beginning to fade; others, that it was not yet ready. The second bottle had no nose, but was longer on the finish. Again, we could not agree. Was it in decline, or did it need five more years? In view of the nose, I thought the former, but we agreed to taste it again in five years' time, during one of Jasper's visits to London.

# ~ The Society of Odd Bottles and the Sisterhood of the Black Pudding ~

The Honourable Society of Odd Bottles has been mentioned in this column before. I can report that the membership is growing. We are now comfortably into low single figures. The other night, the Bottles assembled. At present, we have no lady members, although there is no rule to prevent it. That is hardly surprising. At present, there are no rules. Nor do we usually have a Toast to the Lassies. But despite their absence, we began by discussing women.

We decided that for certain purposes, females could be divided into two groups. There is the voice of duty, and of diet, constantly monitoring their menfolk's intake. Many years ago, when I was a skinny research student, one of my chums had a wife who was a seriously good cook. She also believed in watching his weight. I forget the menu one evening at their place, except the gratin dauphinoise. It was delicious. But the poor husband got a miserable helping of everything else and no dauphinoise. I tried to defend him: 'Come on Liz, Hugh's a big chap. He's not really overweight.' Hope briefly flickered across his features, but was crushed by a low and unwifely blow: 'You haven't seen him in the nude.'

Then there are the girls who believe, despite every evidence to the contrary, that all men are on the point of expiring from hunger. This includes the members of three female clubs who probably do not realise that they are clubs, which is a pity. Otherwise, they could affiliate to the Bottles.

The first are the lady shoppers who assemble daily at Charley Barley's in Stornoway. It purveys the best black pudding in the world and the most salacious gossip in the Western Isles. The first time you arrive, on your way to the airport intending to pick up 20lb or so of black pud, you will be worried. There are at least 20 females in the shop, too long a queue if you are to make your flight. Your fears are unnecessary. You will be ushered straight to the counter while they nod in approval at your order and continue their salty dissection of the neighbours' doings.

The second is a butcher's shop on Smedenstraat, in Bruges. Again, everyone else on the premises is female, and they are talking as vigorously as a club members' table during a good dinner. Once again, you will be beckoned forward, with all the *mevrouwen* listening intently. If you order, say, a Christmas goose, the shop will turn into a seminar, advising you how to cook it. I would always try to take note because, when it comes to cooking, I am a château general. Obviously, one takes the strategic decisions, but the campaign in the kitchen should be left to junior commanders, with plenty of opportunities for female troops.

Third are the girls who run Ai Cugnai, a Venetian restaurant just round the corner from the Accademia. They are tiny creatures with arms the size of chicken bones, but as soon as a man arrives, even one twice their size, there will be a plate of risotto nero, a bicchiere of wine and a debate about which of their dishes is really good today.

One Bottle is fortunate enough to have a French wife. Catherine is altogether a wonderful girl, and a superb cook. She delights in male guests who appreciate what they are eating — hardly an onerous task — especially if they can be relied on to polish off the last confit of duck leg.

At our latest session, we Bottles turned to claret. Are the 2000s justifying their reputation (and price)? The answer is an emphatic yes. We started with a Lanessan: soft, fruity but balanced. No need to keep it; no hurry to finish it off. Then came an Ormes de Pez, which had more power, as one would expect, and was maturing deliciously. It would be a shame to drink it too quickly, for it is not yet quite at its peak. The same is true of the Gloria, which won the prize on the night and had us searching for superlatives. If it is that good, those fortunate enough to possess the greatest names from 2000 have lots of delights in their cellars.

# ~ A toast to all bottles ~

Where two or three British males are gathered together, the agenda often includes a glass or two. One thing can lead on to another. To facilitate the supply of glasses, clubs are sometimes formed. These can vary in size and splendour, from the palaces of Pall Mall to the working men's clubs where the young William Hague delivered beer and sampled the deliveries. (He was unwise to quantify his efforts. It would have been better if he had merely said that from time to time, it was not just the barrels which were rolling.)

There are also clubs within clubs. A couple of us have stumbled into irregular sessions which we have called 'the odd bottles'. The conversation varies: nature conservancy in the Highlands, reactionary politics, the law — the two latter ought to be a distinction without a difference. Even if there are no amusing black cap anecdotes these days, most lawyers are good conversationalists. As Dr Johnson put it, they like folding their legs and having their talk out.

A couple of decades ago, there was a Johnsonian journalist, George Gale. He often held court in the Cheshire Cheese, then a splendidly old-fashioned pub. The Cheese is only round the corner from Gough Square and, one day, a couple of American matrons came in to ask directions. 'Say, could you tell us the way to Dr Johnson's house?' George replied. 'I am Dr Johnson. This is my house. Now fuck off.'

We Bottles convened the other evening. Proceedings started with Hermann Dönnhoff's '07 Riesling Kabinett. Dönnhoff is the best Nahe producer that I have come across, and this was a delight. Though only a Kabinett, it was almost too big for food. Foie gras, perhaps, or a fish pie, but it is a wine designed to be drunk on a misty morning in November, with a slice of fruit cake, overlooking the Rhine. I remember an all-day session in similar circumstances, a few years back. By early evening, I could hear the Rhine Maidens. By late evening, we had moved on to Marc de Gewurztraminer. The next morning, I felt like Alberich.

The Bottles move on, to two absolutely contrasting reds. The first was a d'Issan '05. The year has a great reputation; the wine justified it. It exuded subtlety and class, reminding one of Mitterrand's campaign slogan from 1981: *La force tranquille*. But it would be wrong to do more than sample it now. It has plenty more to give and will last for ever. If you have some in your cellar, congratulate your perspicacity.

That was also true of its successor, an '08 Australian Shiraz, Ladies Who Shoot Their Lunch, from the Strathbogie Ranges in northern Victoria. It had power, as one would expect from the grape and the terroir. You almost think that you can taste the shavings from Ned Kelly's chains. But there was also depth and finesse. This is a wine to watch. I suspect that the girls who make it are on the verge of international fame, and not just because of their exploits with a musket. Indeed, someone proposed electing them to honorary Bottle-hood. There was a vigorous discussion. Can females be Bottles? Would we not be in danger of falling within the Equality Act? We decided ... the truth is that none of us can agree what we decided.

That was partly the fault of the 1960 Dow, which concluded our formal proceedings. It was the owner's last bottle and it had been several years since he had tried it. So some trepidation: 1960 had been a light year, overshadowed by the power and the glory of the '55s and '63s. But it was balanced, harmonious, delicious. We drained the last drops in a toast to all Bottles.

## ~ When it comes to food and wine, there's no place like Rhône ~

As often, a good glass stimulated good talk. We were drinking some promising young Rhônes and the discussion ranged wide, moving onwards from the Rhône itself, to the differences between the UK and our sweet enemy France, then to the merits of democracy and the challenges facing it. Democracy has the overwhelming merit of providing governments with legitimacy, thus ensuring that conflicts are resolved in the legislature rather than on the streets or the battlefield. Though this does not always work — see Germany in the 1930s — it does so often enough to justify the Churchillian maxim: the worst form of government apart from all the alternatives.

Yet there is a problem. If the electoral process is based on PR, governments are likely to be weak. A first-past-the-post system should breed strength, but the danger is that after a narrow result, the minority will sulk off into internal exile, which does not encourage a society to be at ease with itself. We see that in America today and in the UK over Brexit. There is no obvious remedy. Man is a discontented animal, inclined to burden any system of government with a combination of unmeetable expectations and unsustainable contempt. The troubles of our proud and angry dust are usually beyond any politician's therapeutic resources.

One might have thought that this would not apply along the banks of the Rhône. A generation ago, a fellow called Yves Lafoy married Jocelyne. They were both agriculturalists, with a mystical delight in making things grow applied to a shrewd sense of what markets would buy. Skill and ambition led them to wine. Their vineyards are around Ampuis, so they are following in formidable footsteps. After the war, Etienne Guigal founded the house that bears his name. Guigal is especially well-known for its Côte Rôtie. With the help of Robert Parker, who is not always wrong, this has achieved international fame and can command world-class prices, enabling the family to buy the Château d'Ampuis, which bears the rust of medieval wars plus the stylishness of later restorations.

So the Lafoys have an example to spur them to success and rivalry. Their son Gaëtan, now the head vigneron, is enjoying the challenge. Qualified judges think he is one of the finest young winemakers in France. I tasted a couple of his Côte Rôties, from 2015 and 2016. For fruit, structure, style and sophistication, they could not be faulted. All they need is time. We had started with a Condrieu, the supreme expression of the viognier grape. It has been copied all over the world and never remotely equalled. Condrieu matures faster than most serious wines and this one was already pleasant drinking. In another couple of years it will be formidable.

These Lafoys are wines to watch — and they already have been. In London, they are marketed by H2Vin, which delights in pathfinding its way to new growers. They and Gaëtan have a joyous partnership, and the price is still reasonable, especially in comparison with Guigal.

The last time I visited Ampuis, that was a society at ease with itself: so much so that it put the profonde in La France Profonde. There were no great meals, just sound fare based on the traditional cooking of local ingredients: people eating the way their parents and grandparents would have done. The locals could almost have produced their own version of Asterix and Obelix.

In a previous column, I wrote that no one had romanticised the Rhône. Am I in danger of doing so, by implying that the paysage and les fruits de la terre — especially the liquid ones — are an antidote to the human condition? They are certainly a palliative.

# ~ The joy of Glenmorangie ~

Glenmorangie is the most accessible of malt whiskies. It is a gentle, almost feminine creature, with hints of spring flowers, chardonnay, *eine kleine nachtmusik*, wholly different from the lowering malts of the Outer Isles. With them, there is no question of hints, let alone Mozart. A blast of peat and iodine arrives to the skirl of the pipes: a mighty dram worthy of the sea-girt rocks among which it was cradled.

Both have their place. I recently helped a friend polish off his last bottle of '63 Glenmorangie. It had gained in depth, strength and subtlety. Should you possess any, our bottle was showing no scintilla of senescence. Its owner is a Scotsman who has grown rich in the colonies and was resolutely uninterested in his treasure's value (no doubt eye-watering). He claimed that I had earned my share by reassuring him about the referendum campaign. Neither of us could believe that the nation which had invented whisky and provided the staff officers for the British Empire, while also winning glorious battle honours during the Enlightenment, was about to take leave of its senses and vote to girn in a kail-yard.

As we drank, I had a madeleine moment. Back in the late eighties, there was a brief entr'acte when the Green party seemed to be an important political force. They had a conference in Wolverhampton. I went to take a sneer and was not disappointed. There was a balcony of political reporters: every paper had sent a junior political correspondent, tasked with straight coverage. Having listened to hours of tedium, they were on the cusp of mutiny. The Greens had one sole female who would have needed help from the make-up department before going on stage as a witch in *Macbeth*; the rest were beyond parody. I settled on my headline — 'Green Grow the Loonies Oh' — and looked forward to dinner. As an antidote to green cant, I had arranged to entertain a Wolverhampton MP, Nick Budgen.

The late Nick Budgen was a wonderful and impossible fellow. He claimed to have hunted with every pack in England, usually mounted on horses called Hamburger Reject or 'Might Make Dog Food: animals that Flurry Knox would have despaired of coping. But as long as the nag could muster four legs, Nick scorned gates.

He was unlucky in his political timing. For around three-quarters of his career, his party was in government. Nick was preternaturally a man for opposition. So he had to console himself with driving the whips crazy: eventually, he had the whip taken away. On one evening, he found a procedural objection to the Commons' business. He complained to his whip, David Lightbown, an imposing figure who had been a military policeman and a notoriously brutal defender in association football. He was equally notorious for directness of manner. 'I see your game, Budgen. You're trying to make trouble, as usual. You can fuck off.' Budgie then took his grievance to his shop steward, Marcus Fox, the chairman of the '22 Committee. Marcus was very drunk and equally unsympathetic. 'I see your game, Budgen. You're trying to make trouble, as usual. You can fuck off.'

Nick told that story with relish. Few MPs would have been quite so amused when recounting repeated snubbings. Anyway, he and I moved on from a '61 Lynch-Bages to a '63 Glenmorangie. Both found favour.

Everything about Glenmorangie encourages favourable feelings, except the recent behaviour of its advertising department. They have produced a picture of a bottle, with two glasses — full of ice. Ice: the shame of it. There is also a slogan: 'unnecessarily well-made'. That should be one of the stupidest, most pretentious statements in the history of advertising, unless the once-great house of Glenmorangie is now intent on betraying its product. In which case, 'unnecessarily well-made' is the literal and deplorable truth.

## ~ The soul of a lurcher
## and the secret of a capon ~

A county, a house, a dog — and a bottle. Somerset: men have delved and farmed and built here for millennia, reshaping the landscape but never losing harmony with nature. There lies the dearest freshness pretty near the surface of things. My friends live in the Vale of Blackmore, good hunting country, in a prosperous farmhouse. Over the centuries, it has been added to and bashed about. The exterior is Victorian-esque, but I bet that there is medieval masonry at the core of the stouter walls.

In the kitchen, there are oak beams, perfect for hanging hams and flitches of bacon. Indeed, they could be needed for a similar purpose now, because of the dog. El Awrence, a lurcher, is a splendid example of the breed, in his charm, character and relentless criminality. Now that no one in polite society would dream of referring to gypsies as pikeys, the word is left vacant. Perhaps it should be applied to lurchers: pikey-dogs. In El Awrence's case, there is an alternative. He has not yet learned how to co-exist with sheep, to the extent that he almost qualifies as a sheep-hound.

What a monster. But sin does not necessarily mean soullessness. These days, no one seems interested in debating whether animals have souls. If they did, lurchers would provide powerful evidence for the 'yes' camp. For a start, and however mired in evil, they generally manage to look soulful. There is also a clinching theological point. If you do not have a soul, how can you have original sin? Could anyone deny that the lurcher/pikey has a treble dose of ancestral depravity? Ergo, it must have a soul.

El Awrence would look superb if taken hunting in the desert. Even so, I am not sure that it was wise to give him a name which is an incitement to brigandage. I know a girl who used to have a magnificent lurcher called Bandit. That was asking for trouble, and he provided it. Once, staying with her, I carefully left a piece of black pudding to be the final morsel at breakfast. Then I was called away to the phone. Came back: empty plate; innocent-looking Bandit. Although there was murder in my heart, I contented myself with cutting a toast soldier, buttering it thickly with mustard, and leaving it on the plate while I left the room. To begin with, the dog must have thought that I was a real softie, but by the time I returned, he was struggling. In a remarkable feat of canine bravery, he had scoffed half the soldier. The experience neither impaired his digestion nor improved his morals.

At least lurchers do not steal claret. A splendid setting, a house ready to bask in its inmates' enjoyment, dear friends both of whom love cooking: there had to be a worthy bottle. Lunch was spring lamb; dinner, a capon. Why do we not eat much more capon much more often? The French understand its merits. As Christmas approaches, the menus are full of *chapon fermier*. Partly because of turkey's self-evident deficiencies, British foodies have talked up goose: in my heretical view, the praise for that bird is excessive. It would be interesting to know why Falstaff's capon gave way to Bob Cratchit's goose. Give me capon, any time. All you need is a cock-chicken and a sharp pair of nail scissors. If you regard nail scissors as effeminate and your lady refuses to allow hers to be used for that, a cigar-cutter would do the trick, or perhaps the local rabbi could lend a hand.

The merit of a magnum among three is that with superhuman self-restraint, there could be some left for dinner. We had a 1990 Lynch-Bages, en magnum, at the peak of its powers. I think that it was the best claret I have ever drunk which was not a first growth. As we gave the decanter a final despairing squeeze, a fine red sunset was fading through the woodlands. Perfection is rarely so perfect.

# ~ Life and death of a Tokay ~

I was praying for a miracle, but it seemed unlikely. There had been one already: the bottle's very survival. A second would qualify it for sainthood.

It was an extraordinary story, almost on the scale of *The Hare with Amber Eyes*. Towards the end of the Napoleonic wars, a barrel of Imperial Tokay was dispatched from Trieste to St James's St, where it was bottled by Berry Bros, in 1811. From there, a bottle went to St Petersburg, where it rested for more than a century in a well-appointed cellar. In 1917, it ought to have been delicious. Imperial Tokay is an immensely long-lived wine, well capable of making a century. But its possessors forgot the Russian grand duke's dictum: between the revolution and the firing squad, there is always time for a bottle of champagne. Tokay would be an admirable substitute.

The owners fled south, to join White Russians fighting the Bolsheviks. After appalling privations, they lost. But some of them escaped, possibly via Baku on the Black Sea. During all those travails, someone preserved the Tokay in their luggage. Goodness knows why. Amid the bitter waters of defeat, it might have been a comfort. Perhaps it became a talisman. It would be drunk one day, when justice was done and evil overthrown. Until then, it would serve as a memory of a lost life: a symbol of a blighted world.

From Baku or wherever, family members reached Shanghai, still with the bottle. It was not easy to be a White Russian exile. *Hauts bourgeois* became taxi drivers. Some ladies sold their jewellery. For others' sales, see Sonia in *Crime and Punishment*. It was said of female White Russians that they dressed on credit and undressed for hard cash. Yet the bottle survived.

Its owners cannot have been among the brokest of the broke, because they had a Chinese servant. In the early 1940s, fleeing from the Japanese or the Maoists or both, they abandoned Shanghai and left a few belongings behind, including the bottle of Tokay. They may have hoped to return; they may just have overlooked it. There was no return, and their former servant had the bottle when he arrived in Hong Kong, also fleeing, also penniless.

Hard work in a free economy put that right. His grandson is seriously rich and thoroughly cultivated. Determined to rebut the notion that the Chinese are only interested in Lafite from auspicious years, he has sought my advice on wine, and I have responded by sending him to those who really know their stuff. It was the Chinese mid-autumn celebration: as my friend put it, our harvest festival. I was invited, and not only for mooncakes. We were to taste the fruits of earlier harvests: from vineyards. He told me about the Tokay and would not be dissuaded from opening it.

I prayed for a miracle, but am not in good standing with the Almighty. Reason prevailed. The taste: exactly what you would expect from a 200-year-old wine which had spent several decades as a refugee. It was dead. There was a stale nose and it looked muddy in the glass. I let some brush my lips and I think that there was a hint of ghostly honey. But it was gone. Reviving it would have required a second Miracle at Cana.

Pensively, we considered the grandeurs of the 19th century: the stability, the growth of civilisation and prosperity, the harmonious circumstances which made possible that wine's happy evolution. Then we mused on to the horrors of the 20th century. It may be that those long-dead Russians who had preserved the bottle were trying to convey a message for posterity. I asked my friend why his grandfather had held on to the bottle: he regretted his failure to press the same question before the old boy died. Expressing anxiety as to whether it too would have faded, he then produced another wine, a Clos de Vougeot 2000, Domaine René Engel. That deserves a column to itself, which it shall receive.

# ~ Flowers of Scotland ~

Back in the sixties, there was a more than usually sanguinary murder in Glasgow. While the killer was awaiting trial, the Scottish *Daily Express* decided to buy up his family. This must have been after the days when such a case would end with a good hanging; Alan Cochrane insists that he is not that old. But the newspaper thought that the low-lifers' tales of the dark and bloody alleyways of the Gorbals would titillate its readers. Alan, then a young reporter, was told to hide the family from rival bidders until judgment day, in some discreet hotel up on Lomond-side. That did not sound a hard posting, until he met the MacTumshies.

At the first meal, they sat awkwardly on their chairs and gazed suspiciously at the menus — even the ones who were holding them the right way up. Alan tried to accelerate proceedings. 'What about starting with smoked salmon?' 'Ah've no had that,' said Dad: 'Ah'll gie it a go.' It arrived, and the suspicions returned: 'Whaur's the chips?' Then the lawyers panicked. The *Express* was in danger of committing contempt of court. Alan was told to drive the MacTumshies back to the Gorbals, give them 50 quid, and lose them. If they were questioned, there would be little danger of their remembering the name of the paper that had tried to suborn them. Alan insists to this day that he could not have borne another 12 hours in their company.

Those are tales of yesteryear. In this century, even if the Union is under threat, 'Scottish cuisine' is no longer an oxymoron. Gone are the days when 'green vegetable' was only used as an insult to the Catholic Irish: when a Glasgow salad meant a plate of chips. But there is still a deplorable reluctance to exploit Scottish produce. Every week, refrigerated lorries leave the Highlands, bound for Spain. Their cargo — lobsters, crabs, langoustines, scallops — going to those who appreciate them. Shame on the Scots who fail to.

Even when the best ingredients are available, there are frustrations. I once spent a night in an old-fashioned hotel on Islay. Dinner: first course, soup; disgusting. It tasted as if it had come out of a packet, probably of wartime vintage. It may have been made from left-over Woolton pie. Main course: 12 langoustines. They tasted as if they had been alive half an hour earlier. Cooked lightly and succulently, dressed with garlic butter, they would have graced any restaurant in the world. So: what's for pudding? Answer, mousetrap cheese and/or ice cream. Provenance of the ice-cream? Wall's.

Throughout the Highlands, there are hairy English dropouts who vote SNP. They supplement the dole by weaving plaids from their beard clippings and often keep a goat or two. Persuade one of them to turn his hand to Islay chèvre. Induce a neighbouring housewife to make some soup: a Cullen skink or a Scotch broth. Find a girl who could run up a decent crumble. Let ambition vault; fish does not really do as a main course, so what about some venison, or a grouse? Grouse freezes well, as I was pleasantly reminded over dinner on Easter Sunday. When all the game has been scoffed until the new season, there would be local beef: grass-fed, well-hung. Gourmets would cross oceans for such a repast.

But even before our culinary revolution, Islay is vaut le voyage. There is plenty to kill; there is also the whisky coast. Seven miles from the principal town, Port Ellen, is Kildalton Church. Humble, beautiful, solemn and numinous, Kildalton has known prayer for at least 1,200 years. A place for contemplation as twilight falls, it evokes the perilous guard-duty of the Celtic Church, protecting the flickering Christian flame out on the far edge of the known world, menaced by Norse raiders from the sea.

The approach march is more secular, taking you past three distilleries: Laphroaig, Lagavulin, Ardbeg. Even after a long evening comparing and contrasting great whisky, one has to agree that the Scottish Enlightenment is North Britain's greatest contribution to world history. But the Scottish endram-ment is not far behind. I shall return to that theme, when less distracted by sociology, religion or food.

## ~ What it's like to drink
## a 118-year-old wine ~

Marcher country, the Jura lies to the east of Burgundy and the contrast is marked. Burgundy: the very name is redolent of opulence. The architecture, the courtliness, the great wines: the aristocratic civilisation of Burgundy is a dance to the cornucopia of nature. Among the rocks and hills and gorges of the Jura, nature is less generous: livelihoods harder wrought. But as so often in European history, adversity has been the nursery of triumph.

The Jura produces a famous wine, vin jaune. Until this week, I had hardly tasted it. That has now been rectified, in a spectacular manner. Those who try to write about wine often talk of terroir, minerality and tradition. With vin jaune, those are understatements. This is an old-fashioned wine, made as it was centuries ago: tasting as wines of earlier eras probably tasted, when preservation was the first priority.

Left to itself, wine will oxidise and deteriorate. Down the ages, vignerons have striven to prevent that happening. The Jurans found their solution. They allow a degree of oxidisation to occur while the wine is still in the barrel. Around 40 per cent of the wine evaporates during its first seven years, while it ferments under a yeast crust. The result: the longest-lived wine of all.

We started with an adolescent: the 1947. I might have guessed that it was ten or 12 years old. At first acquaintance, one could mistake it for a fino sherry. It is mouth-puckering: there is plenty of acid. Then the flavours fill out: nuts, subtlety, spices — and length. There is a tremendous nose, and the aftertaste goes on for ever. We moved on the 1929, and the vin jaune showed no signs of age. It was in vigorous prime of life.

These wines came from Château Chalon, the finest vin jaune, and from the family cellar of Jean Bourdy. The Bourdy family has been making wine since the 16th century. Rather like a great nobleman planting a new wood for posterity, they have all grown accustomed to laying down wines which their grandchildren will drink, or sell.

Or perhaps that should be great-great grandchildren. The climax was an 1895. The phylloxera infection was slow to reach Jura; this was from pre-phylloxera vines. On first sniff, I thought I detected just a soupçon of mustiness. If so, it was mere bottle-stink from air that had been trapped for over a century. In 1895, Rosebery's brief prime ministerial vintage had just spluttered out, like an ill-made candle. Here was a wine of that same year. I was ready to be sceptical. One wants to drink wine, not a label. A wine of great age obviously arouses curiosity, but what will it taste like?

Doubts and scepticism were instantly dispelled. This was a wine in the plenitude of maturity: a patriarch in age, a paterfamilias in authority. The power, the length; this is a remarkable wine. It is not easy to accommodate with food, or with other wines. It requires — and is entitled to — concentration. An aperitif? Possibly, but leave plenty of time for the last lingering flavour to dissipate. Despite the fino comparison it is not fortified and only clocks about 13 degrees of alcohol. Even so, I think that it would work as a digestif.

How long will it last? Our hosts had a bottle of 1781, which they had recently purchased for £38,000. We were willing them to make a mistake and open it. When last tasted, we were told, the 1781 had been superb. I see no reason to disbelieve it.

Apropos digestifs, our munificent benefactors, Oracle Capital Group, run inter alia a wine investment fund, and they have a magnificent holding of Cognacs. In other hands, wine investment might seem a dubious concept, but David Nathan-Maister and his colleagues are reverent oenophiles. There are moments when it would be fun to be an oligarch.

'The connoisseurs who picked up on a little extra acidity in the flavour from the quinze hectare.'

# ~ Dining in style at David Cameron's favourite Italian ~

It is impossible to think about any Italian region without wondering 'What if?' Sardinia lacks the glamour, grandeur and menace of Sicily, but it is still a fascinating exemplar of Mediterranean culture: the different historical strata stretching back to pre-history. So: what if the mediaeval rulers of Aragon had been more enduring? What if the Catholic kings had never married? There is no reason why Barcelona should have been ruled from Madrid: still less for the Sardinians to be governed by Turin. A sea-girt Aragonese kingdom, including the Languedoc, Sardinia and Sicily — that would have been a glorious flowering of civilisation and romance: Venus emerging from a scallop shell.

The Angevins, driven from the Mediterranean, could have contented themselves with bringing good government to their French domains, subordinated to London. Meanwhile, a Burgundian middle kingdom — a revived Lotharingia under the Hapsburgs — would have been a rival centre of the graces and the arts. All a fantasy, but anyone contemplating the damage which modern Europeans have inflicted on their continent might well seek refuge in fantasy.

Or in a more substantial alternative: a good dinner. Every now and again, David and Samantha Cameron escape from No. 10 for dinner, and they often enjoy Sardinian food and wine at either of Mauro Sanna's restaurants, Olivomare and Olivocarne, in Elizabeth Street, near enough to dart home if there is a crisis in the shop.

I had a Sardinian feast with Mauro the other night, and it was one of the finest Italian meals I have eaten, and drunk. We started with a fortified Sardinian wine, Vernaccia di Oristano 1990, which had a long, slow, pungent, almost musty, even truffled, quality, unlike anything I had encountered. It is something of an acquired taste, which the PM has failed

DRINK!

to acquire. I liked it, and it laid a sound foundation.

As regards food, we began with roast marrowbone, enlivened by a little spice. Then came gnocchi with black truffles. I can still taste them. To follow, steak tartare chopped up with bottarga (grey mullet roe, a Sardinian speciality). That managed to outshine the truffles. It was one of the best things I have ever eaten.

The principal course was to be suckling pig. I was sceptical. The Cecils of Dorset have replaced Lord Emsworth as the great aristocratic patrons of swine-husbandry. About pigs, all there is to know, they know it, and what they don't know isn't knowledge. I have eaten suckling pig with them, and we all confessed to disappointment. Suckling pig sounds as if it should be delicious, but I have always felt that the porker would be better after a few months rootling and fattening among the acorns and beech-mast, enriching the flesh and ensuring succulent crackling. Perhaps a suckling pig ought to be left to suckle a bit longer.

Not Mauro's one. Though it may have been a brief life, none of it was wasted. That little piggy packed a palatory punch. *Periit ante diem* — but for Lucullus. Puddings followed, especially a gelato made out of frozen yoghurt with bitter Sardinian honey.

What did we drink? Plentifully. Over the past few years, Sardinian wine has greatly improved. Cannonau used to be a simple red infuriator, good for reviving frozen winter-fuel gatherers if you had run out of brandy. It now produces serious stuff, as does Vermentino. We tasted a number of bottles, including Mauro's excellent house selections.

The restaurant is run on *Il padrone mangia qui* lines. Mauro is a proselytiser. He and his team delight in bringing Sardinia to the uninitiated. The restaurants would work well for a banquet: the kitchen and the cellar enjoy being put through their paces. But they would work equally well if, like the Camerons, you just wanted to unwind for a couple of hours with excellent food and a decent bottle.

# ~ Enjoying South Africa's secret
# French connection ~

One aspect of the old South Africa's racial policies cannot be faulted. After the revocation of the Edict of Nantes, Huguenot refugees arrived at the Cape. Within a few decades, they had been culturally cleansed, abandoning the French language and becoming decent Afrikaners. If only we had possessed the foresight to do something similar in Quebec. But the immigrants were allowed to retain a legacy of their grenouille past: winemaking skills. They planted vineyards around Franschhoek and Stellenbosch, creating a great oenophile tradition which still flourishes.

The terroirs are in achingly beautiful terrain. Early on my first visit to South Africa, in 1984, I met a chap who had been working in the President's Council — the equivalent of our Cabinet Office — at a senior level, but was giving that up for a chair at Stellenbosch, though he was only in his late thirties. I asked him why the devil he was rusticating himself and got only mumblings for an answer. I ran into him a few weeks later and he looked as if he was about to resume the mumblings. 'No, no,' said I, 'you don't need to explain anything. Since we spoke, I've been to Stellenbosch.'

It is a university town, and on that glorious autumn day, several elevens of Valkyries were cycling back from tennis: the blonde flower of Afrikaner maidenhood, also achingly beautiful. There were young men too, coming back from rugger, with thighs like oak trees. It was surprising that the bikes could bear their weight, and the Springboks were not about to run short of prop forwards. I was with a homosexual colleague. So moved was he by the flower of Afrikaner manhood that I feared we would all be arrested.

The academics of Stellenbosch were also a source of flowering. Although history will be reluctant to give them credit, André du Toit,

Willie Esterhuyse and their friend Wimpie de Klerk played a crucial role in creating a new dispensation in Afrikanerdom. I remember many evenings in the gardens of Stellenbosch. We all agreed that the blacks should have the right to full human dignity, immediately. There should be economic equality of opportunity and an extensive programme of educational uplift, immediately. Blacks should have equal rights in local government, immediately. State power: there, consensus was harder. How could the necessary fundamental change be achieved without chaos? The debates went backwards and forwards, fruitlessly. F.W. de Klerk — Wimpie's brother — was clear-sighted enough to see that the answer was not to be found in niceties. There was no alternative to a leap in the dark.

While deciding the future of South Africa, we often drank the wines of Kanonkop, a distinguished Stellenbosch domain. It produces excellent cabernet sauvignon but also pinotage, a South African cross between pinot noir and cinsault. One evening in Jo'burg, giving dinner to Bill Deedes, I ordered some South African wines, including a seriously old and excellent pinotage, imagining that he would enjoy the fruits of my recent expertise. A couple of nights later, I was disabused. A return match, and it became clear that the Deedes' palate was firmly grain-based. Wine was something you drank with food, to cover the interval between gin and Scotch.

Over the weekend, I renewed my acquaintance with Kanonkop. We had the Pinotage Black Label 2010, far too young but full of power and promise. The same was true of a Cabernet Sauvignon 2008, which I would have taken for a wine from the Médoc. It needs at least another couple of years.

My friends had suffered a flood in their cellar, which destroyed a lot of labels. We had a pinotage and a Paul Sauer — predominantly cab. sauv., but with some merlot and cabernet franc — both from the mid-1990s, both superb. Because of the weak rand, Kanonkop is excellent value. Look out for its wines, especially with some bottle age.

# ~ When an economist turns into a winemaker ~

My friend Mitch Feierstein is a jolly, cheerful, life-enhancing fellow. He is emphatically not one of those economists whose purse-lipped response to any new phenomenon is 'no good will come of this' and who have predicted six of the past two recessions. But he is a profound pessimist. In a book he published last year, *Planet Ponzi*, he devotes page after relentless page to the troubles of the world economy. He depicts the West as a ship without engine or rudder, adrift on a sea of bad debt, worse paper and wholly unrealistic expectations. It is even gloomier than the voyage of the Ancient Mariner. He at least found redemption.

There may be only one way out. Perhaps a global 'bad bank' could corral all the valueless paper and gradually write it away, without producing hyperinflation and destroying the few surviving moral underpinnings of the international financial system. Perhaps. In the short run, like the Russian grand duke, Mitch believes that between the revolution and the firing squad there is always time for a bottle of champagne. In a dog Latin paraphrase, *e pessimus vinum*. Mitch has invested in Tuscan vineyards, around Borgo la Casaccia.

Vinous Tuscany resembles Burgundy, in that the arts and crafts of viticulture have been practised there for millennia. Ancient churches are often numinous, as if the stones were infused with centuries of prayer. Ancient vineyards have a similar quality, as if the earth and the vines are also infused, with the graces of long civilisation.

Tuscan hill villages share in all that. There is a delicious sense that the pace of life has accommodated itself to the seasons of the grape. You go into one, intending to transact some business with the *avvocato*. He is not in his office, so you decide to call on the *dottore*. He is not there either, so suspicion turns into certainty. There they both are, sitting in the shade outside Beppe's, on to their second glass of Toscano Bianco, a modest little wine, made locally for family and fun, in corners of vineyards principally devoted to the grandeurs of sangiovese. There can often be a problem with these local wines. They will taste delicious under a trellis of vine leaves, overlooking the swimming pool. They will not work so well on a wet Monday in a London November. But a Toscano Bianco will travel, and taste a lot better than many a sauvignon blanc. The difficulty lies in persuading the locals to part with it.

The *avvocato* and the *dottore* assure you that there is nothing wrong with your finances or your health. This is not the time for further and better particulars. There is certainly nothing wrong with the wine, and the hints from the kitchen are beginning to entice. It smells as if Beppe will be on form today, and your professional advisers concur: there is an urgent need to see how the 2009 reds are doing.

The wines of La Casaccia are only just beginning to reach the UK. Just below Sloane Square, there is a restaurant called Como Lario. Years ago, it used to be the sort of Italian where the 'Chianti' bottles wore straw jackets and the waiters pranced around with four-foot pepper dispensers. It was then transformed by a group of investors including Adrian Ziani de Ferranti, a descendant of the Ziani doges who held office around the end of the first millennium, and whose bodies are buried under the pavement of the crypt of San Zaccaria. Today, Como Lario serves serious scoff. A dish of linguini with spring truffles was unsurpassable, and La Casaccia's 2008 Brunello was the perfect accompaniment. Even without truffles, the wines are excellent. They will become more available in the UK and are worth a search.

# ~ When Glyndebourne is the most perfect place on earth ~

Glyndebourne. There is no single quintessential example of English scenery, but this is one of the finest. The landscape is old, and verdant. There has been tillage and pasturage here for millennia, and the outcome is harmony, as if tamed nature has embraced man's gentle mastery. On a sunny summer evening, earth has not anything to show more fair.

*Figaro.* Anyone reading the libretto might conclude that earth had not anything to show more absurd. What is this nonsense: a Feydeau farce mitigated by a bit of carpentry? There is a simple answer: the best of all comedies, apart from Shakespeare — and more easily, more continually laughter-worthy than even *Love's Labour's Lost, A Midsummer Night's Dream* or *Twelfth Night.* In a proper production of *Figaro*, there should be an almost constant susurration of chuckling.

The current Glyndebourne production passes that test. The spectre of Graham Vick has been exorcised. Once again, Mozart is beautiful. There are eccentricities. The Page ought to be a small volcano of priapism. The Countess, Susanna, Barbarina: even Marcellina is barely safe from his attentions. But this one makes Voi che sapete sound melancholy. Susanna is a delightful little scamp, but the scene in which she and the Countess undress Cherubino, to re-equip him with female garments, should be sexier. Equally, why is it — not just in this production — that Barbarina always looks so much like her father?

But those are quibbles. In *Figaro*, the comedy is scintillating, the music, the most sublime ever written. Lord, what fools these mortals be.

On Sunday, after the usual fizz, Sancerre and other pleasantries, we graced the strawberries with a bottle of Coutet '96. It added perfection to perfection. One is intellectually aware that an Yquem of the same vintage would be even finer, but that is merely another quibble. That bottle was an ideal way of tying all the threads together: the opera, the laughter, the glory of the music, the beauty of the countryside: all captured in a glass.

I am not sure that one should admit it, but the French do have their uses. Until phylloxera struck in the mid-19th century, Langlade, near Nimes, produced highly regarded wine. After the plague, everything seemed extinct. Deserted villages decayed in the midst of mouldering vines. Where man had planted, laboured, harvested, bottled and revelled, the grazing was abandoned to goats and donkeys.

But in the late 1990s, Rémy Pedreno, a successful businessman, came to Langlade, looked around him, and stroked his chin. He has Spanish roots and a matador's temperament. He does not lack confidence or chutzpah. He has revived the wines, now known as Roc d'Anglade. For his red, the principal grape is carignan, blended with grenache, mourvedre and syrah. He also produces a white and a rosé, neither of which I have tried. I am confident that the white will be excellent. As for the rosé, if he is prepared to give it his imprimatur, I will overcome my deep-lain prejudices.

Rémy himself only cultivates 25 acres, because he is striving for the highest standards. I tasted his 2008, '09 and '10. Although there was nothing the matter with the '08, the two later vintages were superb. The '09 will drink now, but will also keep. The '10 is full of promise. Other vignerons are now moving to Langlade. I have never understood the appellation rules, but this is a name to conjure with, especially when Escamillo — or rather Rémy — is the producer.

Poor old France. The wretched, feeble Hollande has achieved the impossible. There is now a nostalgia for his predecessor. Come back, Sarko: even if all is not exactly forgiven, you could hardly do any worse. But Rémy Pedreno and Roc d'Anglade offer consolation. There is an eternal France, which transcends the politicians.

# ~ Mourning Julia Gillard with the greatest wine ever to come out of Australia ~

My Australian friend was in mourning over the removal of Julia Gillard, the country's first female prime minister. She had been everything a leftist politician ought to be: ineffectual and un-electable. I concurred; sacking Labour leaders just because they could not win an election sets a very bad example to the rest of the world.

For solace, he had decanted a bottle. Something in the nonchalance with which the glass was poured aroused my suspicions, which were strengthened when the nose reached halfway across the room (he is, shall we say, well off). I sipped, savoured splendour, and speculated. 'I think I've had this before, to celebrate when a girl called Mary Wakefield joined *The Spectator*. It wasn't quite ready then. It is now.' Robert Parker said that once mature, the '76 Grange Hermitage would rival the '61 Pétrus, which I have never tasted. It is possible to question Mr Parker's judgment on cab. sauvs grown in gravelly soil, but he is at ease with more instantly accessible wines. The King of Shiraz and the Queen of Merlot: a happy comparison.

That said, there is a caveat for any squillionaire tempted to arrange such a courtship. At a plutocratic dinner party in Manhattan, another friend of mine was recently served a '69 Le Montrachet and the '61 Pétrus. What, apart from envy, did I think? 'The Pétrus ought to have been beyond praise while the Montrachet had an excuse for showing its age. But I'm obviously meant to be counter-intuitive, so presumably it was vice-versa.' 'Bang on. The Montrachet tasted as if it would last for ever, but even the Yanks could tell that the Pétrus was disappointing.' Equally, another friend of mine, Robin Bomer, whose cellar rivals his palate, says that he has occasionally run a Grange Hermitage against a Hermitage la Chapelle from a good but not great vintage. The northern hemisphere has always prevailed.

Even so, that '76 was the finest Rhône-ish wine that I have ever tasted: apart from soldiery in time of war and need, the finest thing to come out of Australia not wearing a baggy green cap and carrying a cricket bat. I was feeling sufficiently generous to commiserate with my chum about this year's Ashes vintage. We moved on to philosophy. Two rugger matches, each fought like an excerpt from the Battle of the Somme: each decided by a missed kick. What if the third game went the same way? Like the Huns in 1918, neither side would accept that it had lost. We agreed that a draw might be preferable to a one-point win — and that a try should earn seven points.

Still on sport, and in consolation for La Gillard, we discussed Wimbledon and solved the problem of sexism. Some Neanderthals are still arguing that it is wrong to pay women as much as men. What nonsense — but it is time to push the feminist agenda further. In this era of equality, what possible justification is there for two competitions? Let us sweep away this segregation, and create a truly enormous prize. I do not know why Harriet Harman has not proposed this already.

A small percentage of the monies could be kept back, to create a spectacle for the spectators' idle amusement. While their sisters were slaughtering the men on Centre Court, any lesser girls who were eliminated early could play each other over three sets. But in this minor event, the tennis would not be the sole factor. There would have to be a looks test as well. The aim would be to ensure that pretty girls in frilly dresses were scampering around the court: a perfect accompaniment to a glass of Pimm's. Feminine squealing would be permitted, but only up to a certain decibelage, falling well short of sounding like Molly Bloom on LSD. Grunting would, of course, be banned. Now that she is *désoeuvrée*, Julia Gillard might like to present the trophy. As we finished the last drops of Grange, we sought a name for the new competition, firmly rejecting the Frilly Fillies' Stakes — and arrived at the obvious solution: the Gillard–Harman Cup.

## ~ A lord's prayer ~

There was a splendid old fellow called Ian Winterbottom, successively a Yorkshire businessman, a Labour MP and a junior defence minister in the Lords (he later joined the SDP). He was the sort of Labour supporter who dismays Tories, because his politics were based on social generosity. It would have been impossible to dismiss him as an extremist. He was universally popular in the Lords, though sometimes his private office could have crowned him.

When he was due to answer questions, the office staff always gave him a full briefing; they were good at predicting awkward questions and supplying emollient answers. All the minister had to do was read out his crib. But dear old Ian often decided to strike out on his own. He would return to safety by saying that he would write to the Noble Lord; and his office would have to draft a letter. Apart from that, he was the easiest boss imaginable.

Until the crisis. The government was closing a shore-based naval establishment: a name like HMS *Primrose*. Some peer was bound to raise the question of redundancies; they were inevitable. But there was no reason for Ian to sound callous. The draft was as follows: 'I am grateful to the Noble Lord for raising that point and I can assure him that my Rt Hon. friend the Secretary of State will keep the matter under close review.' Instead, when asked whether he could assure the House that there would be no redundancies, Ian replied: 'Yes, my Lords, I am happy to give that assurance.'

Consternation. Before Ian had sat down, his private secretary had sprinted up the back stairs to plead with the Hansard writers. They were obdurate; they could not change 'yes' into 'no'. There was only one hope. The distressed official went to beg mercy from Lord Denham, the Tory chief whip. If the answer stood, Lord Winterbottom would have to resign. 'We can't have that,' said Bertie Denham. 'We're all very fond of Ian.' So a

Tory chief whip rode to the rescue of a Labour minister. According to Hansard, Lord Winterbottom said: 'No, my Lords, I regret that I cannot give such an assurance.'

In Ian's presence, I was once guilty of a failure of journalistic persistence. He had just come back from a trip to Japan. As a peer and a minister, he was well entertained. At one dinner, there was not only a geisha girl to charm him at the table. There was a girl available for later on. Ian knew the score. On their expenses, his hosts could claim for the level of entertainment he had enjoyed, but no more. If he went off with a girl, they could do likewise, on the company. Otherwise, they had to pay for their own. 'Quite a dilemma,' Ian twinkled. I failed to ask how he resolved it.

Ian has an equally impressive son, Dudley Winterbottom. He used to run the Cherwell Boathouse in Oxford: simple food, excellent wine. The first time I dined *chez* Dudley, I ordered a bottle which he had not tried. 'D'you mind if I have a glass?' He then brought a different, equally interesting bottle. So it went on all evening. A lot was drunk. Financial caution floated away down the Cherwell. I was bracing myself for a stonker of a bill, and when it arrived, I did complain. 'This is ridiculous, Dudley. It can't cover the historic cost of what my lot have polished off, never mind the food. We did eat something, between glasses.'

Dudley went on to be secretary of the Chelsea Arts Club, a raffish compromise between St James's and Bohemia. I was there the other day, to learn about Argentine wines. My friend Anthony Foster, MW, produced a bottle of 1982 Rafael, a cabernet sauvignon. It was delicious. He had come across two bottles, long-forgotten survivors, and opened one at Christmas to use as mulled wine. He tasted it to ensure that it was still drinkable, and realised from the nose alone that it was far too good for mulling. The fruits of my further Argentine researches will await another occasion. Suffice for now: that benighted nation is far, far better at viniculture than politics.

# ~ The tastes of temptation ~

There ought to be a wise adage: 'If invited to do good works, always procrastinate. A better offer is bound to turn up.'

About a month ago, the phone rang. Would I attend the Oxford vs Cambridge wine tasting, sponsored by Pol Roger, which would also include a wine hacks vs wine trade contest? Festivities were to continue over lunch. The likelihood of a wooden spoon did not deter me. I was joyously accepting, when a horrible thought occurred. I checked the diary. My forebodings were justified. I was already engaged, to speak at the King's School, Bruton.

There was one possible solution: do both. Get thee behind me, Satan. There could be worse embarrassments than finishing last in a tasting. I had no wish to emulate Gussie Fink-Nottle's oration to the Market Snodsbury Grammar School. I remember overhearing Willie Whitelaw back in 1979 on his plans for the election campaign. As ever, there was a minuscule pause between his pronouncements. 'I have made it clear ... that I shall be very happy ... to go up and down the country ... speaking for Conservative candidates ... as long as they give me four glasses of whisky before I start.' (Willie's glasses owed nothing to pub measurements.) 'If they give me more than four glasses, I shall still be happy to go on the platform ... but I hope that someone will prevent me.'

Duty prevailed. I stepped westward, to a splendid evening. Impressive and charming headmaster: ditto his staff; bright, delightful kids who did not seem depressed by 40 minutes of geopolitical pessimism and fought back with probing questions. There was only one problem. I know lots of stories, any of which would be fine for a rugger club after a good dinner — but mixed company? That said, the young these days are almost certainly the least shockable people in any room. Even so, the head, Ian Wilmshurst, censored one anecdote which seemed innocent enough to me.

It was about education. Every year, Tonbridge School used to take its lower sixth to Coventry, for a real-world tasting. The boys would visit comprehensives, meet the social services and so on (sounds like the worst punishment a school could inflict since the demise of flogging). At the end there was a panel discussion, which included me. I felt that after all the do-gooding guff, the boys needed a sharpener. 'I hope you now understand why you are in Coventry. Although I don't want to be too patronising, boys of your age can be susceptible to idealism. Before you arrived, you might have wondered whether it was right that you should have such a first-rate education, just because your fathers can afford the fees. But you have been here for a week. You have met the caring workers, the sharing workers and the other outlets for public spending. You will have drawn the obvious conclusion. There is a Darwinian dimension to your presence at Tonbridge. It is not just about cash. It is about genetic superiority.'

There was plenty of that in the wine-tasting which I missed. It included a '95 Haut-Brion, reckoned to be the star performer. But a 2006 Vosne-Romanée 1er Cru Aux Malconsorts, Dujac, was a strong second. I suspect that while today's great clarets succeed in emulating their predecessors, the Burgundians may be surpassing theirs. There was a Le Montrachet from the enchanting 2008 vintage. I am assured that it was forward enough to be enjoyable now, though it must surely have a lot more to say.

A '53 Vega Sicilia is said to have foxed the tasters. I have only been at the drinking of two bottles of that wine. On neither occasion could I see why it was so highly prized. This one had that raisiny, vanilla taste of old rioja, which might have sparked a happy guess. Anyway, it was clearly a magnificent event — except that Oxford won. I am sorry that I was not present, but I am not sorry that I went to Bruton.

## ~ Horse and bourbon ~

At a club table, a group of us was discussing horse-eating, marvelling at the confusion and sentimentality of our fellow countrymen while telling hippophagic anecdotes. I mentioned a typically Provençal street market in Apt. There had been a group of horses. They were not looking happy. More intelligent than Boxer on his way to the knacker's, they clearly sensed that the good days were over and were summoning reserves of stoicism to help them through the (brief) final phase. 'What's going to happen to those horses?' inquired an English female member of the party. 'Well, er, it is either the Sunday Joint Derby or the Hamburger Cup.' 'Oh no, I can't bear it.' I tried to console her by pointing out that in France, clapped-out old nags at least had the privilege of joining the human food chain. In the UK, it would have been the dog-food stakes (or so one then thought).

Strangely enough, she was not comforted. Half the girls spent half the night working out ways to bring those horses back to an honoured asylum in England; thus did Cordelia plan Lear's final retirement. It did not help matters when someone revealed that I had bought both *saucisson d'âne* and *saucisson de cheval* from a stall, although I expressed doubts about the âne. 'Every Provençal market overflows with the stuff,' I said, 'but you never see any donkeys in the fields.' 'That's because they've all been eaten by heartless monsters like you,' came the quick and obvious rejoinder. 'Even so, there ought to be paddocks full of young Eeyores braying, regardless of their doom: scoffing grass and, one hopes, the odd apple to fatten themselves up for next year's *saucisson* harvest.'

The argument grew in vehemence. 'If you'd eat horse, why not dog?' 'I have eaten dog, in China. Wasn't very good. Stick to horse.' 'The thought of eating horse violates my emotions.' 'Have you never stroked a tiny abandoned lamb while giving it its bottle? Lambs are jolly good eating.' 'No one ever rides lambs.' 'Tell that to the Welsh.' 'I'm glad you're now equating eating horses with bestiality.'

Thus it continued, over an excellent dish of *blanquette de veau*. In an attempt to change the subject, a peacemaker asked why veal tasted better in France than in England. I explained why, pointing out that calves are a) creatures of habit and b) not that bright. If they are brought up in a cardboard box and never learn anything about exercise or daylight, why should they miss what they have never experienced? The mind is its own place. That said, I believe that a *blanquette* requires a different style of veal — but the graduates of cardboard college do have a translucent flesh, excellent for soaking up sauces. There were further lamentations. One was forced to conclude that three-quarters of the British people are vegetarian carnivores.

Back in Clubland, we tried to define the difference between horse and beef. As is generally agreed, horse is sweeter, but, though perfectly palatable, it lacks the strength and flavour of well-hung, grass-fed beef. Horse is ideally designed for hamburger — I wonder how much beef finds its way into the average French *steak haché* — but it could never replace Aberdeen Angus. I came up with, I think, the ideal comparison; horse is to beef what bourbon is to whisky. There are decent bourbons. They make an excellent toddy; they work in the right cocktail. But run even a rare, expensive bourbon against a modest malt (inasmuch as there is such a thing) and Scotland wins easily. Like horse, bourbon is too sweet.

I once gave a bottle of good bourbon to my friend Alan Cochrane. He told me that it had been very popular, among the younger set. Enough said. Let the young eat horse, and restrain nonsensical sentimentality. Let them drink bourbon while gradually finding their way to real whisky. For the interim, this will relieve some of the pressure on their elders' supplies.

# ~ Off the wagon ~

Like half of London, I gave the new year a surly greeting. It was time to diet. There are two sorts of diets. First, the ones that may work for girls. Breakfast: part of a lettuce leaf. Lunch: the leftovers from breakfast. Supper: some cottage cheese with watercress. Second, boys' diets, which all concentrate on avoiding carbohydrate. That is not easy. We all enjoy sinking our gnashers in a warm bread roll, liberally buttered, and good pasta is a culinary glory. That said, *il faut souffrir pour être beau* — and at least with a high-protein diet you can have something to eat.

There is a downside. The boys' regimes all involve cutting out grog, at least for a penitential mini-Lent. By boxing and coxing between Atkins and Dukan, choosing from each at his most permissive, I decided that ten drinkless days could suffice. (Dukan is an encouraging fellow, whose text is full of military metaphors. The Frogs could have done with him in 1940.)

I persevered and only found one difficulty, which relates to the theory of evolution. The sceptics will argue that if the evolutionists were right, pussycats would have worked out how to open the fridge door. I had a relevant experience. At a table with a bottle of red wine, my right arm would stretch across to it, unbidden, as if it had learned to evolve — and then had to be called to order by the nervous system's high command. I imagine that a lot of Krauts had a similar problem after the war. At public gatherings, their right arm would leap aloft until the left arm restrained it.

Then I fell. It was a dinner party, on the eighth dry day. On arrival, I confessed that I was off booze, and even declined a glass of champagne, to my hosts' amazement. They said that we were drinking Chablis followed by St-Joseph. 'Get thee behind me, Satan,' was my staunch reply. The husband added, wistfully, that some of it would keep for tomorrow. His tone stimulated me to inquire what exactly would keep for the morrow. He told me that he had sent most of an uncle's cellar to auction, to turn into school fees, which are the curse of today's drinking classes. The amount of good stuff which is now being exported to Hong Kong and Beijing in order to pay for education is a testimony to the squirearchy's selflessness. But the auctioneers had been discouraging about various oddments, including a bottle of '55 port, Taylor's no less. They would sell it if he insisted, but an odd bottle would not command much of a price. So he kept it and had decanted it, in expectation of my presence.

What could one say? After all, modern churchmen no doubt deplore this anti-Satan stuff. It smacks of horn-ism and tail-ism, perhaps even of racism, and Hell is probably no more than a run-down inner-city housing estate, still suffering from Thatcher's cuts. Equally, it would be wrong to drink the port on an empty stomach. So I reconciled myself to the white and the red (was there any of the champagne left?).

The port was as good as it should have been. A lot went wrong in Britain during the seventies and eighties, not least the premature drinking of vintage port. In clubs, the '55s were being thrust into action while still in their juvenescence, to fill the gaps in the front-line caused by the exhaustion of the '45s. So the '55s ran out before they were fully ready, to be succeeded by the equally premature '63s. Thus it went on, to the '77s, which have mostly been drunk before they were in their prime. To judge by that bottle, the Taylor's '55 is now at its peak. Within five years, it may begin a slow and gentle descent. But it is a very high peak. A rich and sonorous wine, it put the Chablis and St-Joseph in their context. Nothing the matter with either, yet there is a hierarchy — and, inshallah, there will always be another opportunity to diet.

## ~ Waters of life ~

Even though they efface the landscape, the snows of midwinter make the deeper symbolism more apparent. The psychic differences between the Northern and the Southern Kingdoms, which long predate Alex Salmond, are most explicit in this season.

When I was a child, Christmas Day was not a bank holiday in Scotland. It was celebrated, but only as a trial match for the major event: Hogmanay. No one has satisfactorily explained its etymology, but the word is so appropriate. It has a moral onomatopoeia. Christmas: despite the best efforts of commerce, it has not lost contact with its origins as the greatest festival of all. Wassailing, merry gentlemen — merry everyone — punch, porter and port, great heartening fires, while the weather is a mere decoration: 'comfort and joy' may come from one of the shallower carols, but it expresses the English Christmas ethos.

Hogmanay is pre-Christian, and has no savour of the New Testament; the Scots have always preferred the Old. At Hogmanay, the elements cannot be expected to behave just because there is a star in the sky and the church bells are ding-donging merrily (an even shallower carol). Untamed, nature must be defied. As if to give the forces of darkness time to muster, a proper Hogmanay does not start until midnight. Thereafter, it is blackavised men struggling along snowy byways, bearing lumps of coal and bottles of whisky. Whisky's etymology is Gaelic. At Christmas, the English have the way, the truth and the life. At Hogmanay, the Scots have the water of life.

What a water it can be. Recently, I had the pleasure of drinking a bottle of Ardbeg, Committee Reserve. I have never had a finer whisky, and rarely tasted a more expensive one. The Island malts have their detractors. I once heard them described, by a man who is normally sound, as tasting like creosote strained through peat. Although that is rank philistinism, there is an asperity; the first taste is not gentle. I could be persuaded that the normal 17-year-old Ardbeg would benefit from longer in barrel, though one understands the demands of cash-flow. With the Committee Reserve, strength has matured into subtlety: the power is immense, but harmonious.

We were talking about old whiskies, so I told a tale of Brussels during the late eighties and a restaurant offering '53 Macallan as an aperitif. That caught my eye as an admirable digestif, especially as it was the same price as a moderate Cognac. The first two glasses arrived with ice. We explained that in Scotland, ice in whisky was a criminal offence. While those drams recuperated, we had another couple, and came to the obvious conclusion. Leaving any of that magnificent whisky at the mercy of foreigners who might subject it to abominable indignities: it would be like leaving a wounded man on Afghanistan's plains.

So we finished the bottle and casually inquired if they had any more (not, I stress, to drink there and then). No, that had been the only one, specially opened for us. It also turned out to have been specially bottled for the Coronation. If one had possessed the foresight to purchase it unopened, it could probably now be exchanged for a case of the Committee Reserve.

There was one trivial problem. I had not been thirsty by the time we started on the whisky, and at nine the next morning I had a briefing with Arthur Cockfield, then one of the UK commissioners. The Arthurian legend had an infallible command of detail. The nickname was misleading, for he did not have the mien of *rex quondam, rex futurus*. He was more like an ancient lizard, and had a relentlessly desiccated voice. One could have done with a more mellifluous companion, especially as he did not offer me so much as a cup of coffee. By the end of the hour, my throat had turned into sandpaper and I needed any old water, urgently, before I could savour in juxtaposition the Arthurian comedy and the previous night's usquebaugh.

# ~ Progress in a bottle ~

Not all change is for the worse. Go into any supermarket in search of an urgent bottle of wine, and you will find a range of respectable bottles at reasonable prices. The buyers are experts and they drive hard deals with the suppliers: large orders for low profit margins. A club wine committee on which I serve was once looking for a house Chablis. Our stoutly old-fashioned members have not caught up with the current market and still expect to pay very little for an acceptable drop of petit Chablis. After tasting some cheap but lamentable bottles, composing fierce missives to the wine merchants who were to blame, and wishing that the cat or horse which they employed in their Chablis plant would have an early and final trip to the vet, we ended up buying some from Tesco. Once relabelled, it served its purpose. The other Christmas, that same chain had a presentable St-Joseph for under a fiver a bottle. It raced off the shelves. I wished that I had bought a lot more.

Think back a generation, to the socially insecure British middle classes, wishing to find a way to wine-drinking but terrified of making fools of themselves, along a route beset by snobbery. In many cases, the chosen route was indeed folly: Blue Nun, Liebfraumilch, Mateus Rosé — and the worst of all, Beaujolais nouveau. That took in people who really ought to have known better.

There was a further malign consequence. I am about to write something which will shock most of my readers. Even so, I shall persevere. Decent wine is made in Beaujolais. Fleurie, Moulin-à-Vent, Morgon: choose with care, and you should find a perfectly competent bottle. Last week, I came across one which was more than competent. A 2009 Chiroubles from Daniel Bouland, it would have benefited from decanting and from another year's ageing. I was trying to work out what it was, until one of my fellow-tasters blurted out the secret before I said anything. I was grateful, because that saved me from a wilderness of erroneous guesses.

Wine tastings can be a trial, if your name begins with 'A'. There will come a moment when you have to taste blind, and then read out your speculations, in alphabetical order. If you are me, you then envy the facility of the Irishman at the wine-tasting in Burgundy.

It was organised by one of the leading houses, and they had invited the eminences of the British wine-writing trade. But someone's Rolodex had slipped and an invitation found its way to a man from the *Ballygobeen Bugle*. The agriculture correspondent, he was also ex officio the wine correspondent. The atmosphere was hushed, reverential. The great ones were sniffing, sipping and spitting. They would occasionally make a furrowed-browed note. He was swigging and swilling and shoving out his glass for more. He did not make notes. He did chortle. His spittoon stayed dry.

The Burgundians were growing thin-lipped. This did not inhibit his geniality. Finally, pouring him more wine through gritted teeth, one of the hosts said: 'I do not know why we are giving you zis, M'sieu. You clearly do not appreciate what you are drinking.' 'Ho no, Sorr. Yer wrong there. I may not have the lingo like these grand ladies and gentlemen, but I'm enjoyin mesel. Why, Sorr, dat last glass: it was like havin' an angel pissin' down yer troat.' The Burgundians were instantly appeased. Even finer bottles were opened. There was talk of renaming his favourite 'le Cuvée de pisse des anges'. I do not think that my wine-tasting efforts will ever receive a similar benediction.

# ~ Queen of Burgundy ~

I sniffed and sipped and concentrated. It was a wine to savour, drop by drop. A Grands Echézeaux '98 from the Domaine de la Romanée-Conti, this was not a mere bottle. It was an epiphany.

'Great hatred, little room': so Yeats summarised Irish history. We could paraphrase him for the DRC: great prices, little room. The clan chief, Romanée-Conti itself, is only four acres; one wonders what every grape is worth. For a chance to buy the wine, at more than £1,000 a bottle en primeur, you virtually have to be entered on a waiting list at birth.

I have only drunk it once. It was in the early eighties at the Plough in Clanfield, Oxfordshire, where the wine list included a 1965 Romanée-Conti for £30. That was a hell of a price for a Burgundy from a bad year. Yet even in those days, it was a bargain for a Romanée-Conti. Did it live up to its reputation? No. I remember it as being drinkable, but nothing special.

A poor vintage is no basis for judgment. But I have heard serious Burgundians grumble about Romanée-Conti. One, who had assisted in the drinking of a couple of bottles from sound years, said that he did not know what the fuss was about. Good? Certainly. Great? Almost. Worth the price? Never. If you could exchange a single bottle of Romanée-Conti for a case of Chambertin-Clos de Bèze, do so.

Whatever the exchange rate for the Grands Echézeaux, I would be reluctant to take it. It was the most feminine wine I have ever drunk. Silken, coy, insinuating and witty, it released its charms with a gracious irony. Gentle reader, if that strikes you as absurd, you should have been alongside me striving to find words to do justice to the occasion. Even as the final droplets danced from glass to palate, that wine had a twinkle in its eye — and was asserting its intellectual equality with those who were drinking it.

In the conversation after the miraculous draught of Grands

Echézeaux, we agreed that the EU was not wholly bad. Pinot noir is a truculent grape. It does not readily express its femininity in joyous compliance. Like Tam o' Shanter's beldame, it can nurse its wrath to keep it warm. Over the centuries — though never in the DRC — the men who had to make their living by taming this shrewish creature resorted to expedients. If the grapes did not produce enough fruit, add some from another source.

The Hermitaged Lafite school of Burgundy-making produced some outstanding wine. Then along came the EU and demanded botanical purity. If a wine claimed to be made from pinot noir, nothing else was permissible. There were protests, from those of us who were accustomed to the heavy, almost black Burgundies of the *ancien regime*. We were wrong.

There had always been Burgundian houses who respected their own grapes in their native terroir. Partly due to improvements in viniculture, others have joined them. Burgundian pinot noir has improved and is improving, which is just as well, given the price of claret. I cannot see why experiments should be prohibited. If Burgundians wish to blend pinot noir with other grapes, why not — as long as the details are on the label. But there may be a good reason why this should be banned. There might not be enough pinot noir to go round.

Claret or Burgundy? I always associate claret with the Scottish Enlightenment: the wine that David Hume and Adam Smith would have offered one another. Its minerality is the perfect accompaniment to an Edinburgh east wind. Burgundy is a south-wind wine: gentle zephyrs, warm arms, a boudoir with a satin lining. Claret: the great intellects of 18th-century Edinburgh in rigorous discussion. Burgundy: Rabbie Burns in pursuit of houghmagandie.

What I am struggling to say is this. That '98 Grands Echézeaux was wondrous.

## ~ Mature consideration ~

It started with a '99 Margaux, which commanded general agreement from the Brits around the table. Nose, length, balance, harmony: all delectable. It was a velvety, feminine wine, full of promise. Even so, the home team concluded, it was not really ready. The Frenchman in our company could not have disagreed more. 'You English — you are a nation of necrophiliacs. This wine is excellent; how could you say that it isn't ready?' I gave battle. As the fruit and the tannins had not fully come together, we were only drinking 70 per cent of the wine. Give it another three or five years, and they would make love in an ecstatic consummation.

The Grenouille shook his head. *'Pauvres Rosbifs*; you come from the cold North and you can never escape it. You don't know how to enjoy yourselves. You think you like wine, but you make it an arid subject surrounded by technicalities. You turn the joys of the sun and the South into a Presbyterian religion. Read Ronsard; learn to embrace the pleasures of the day. Five years: we might all be dead.' At that moment, an enchanting young girl glided by, shyly — and slyly? — aware that she was the cynosure of every eye. *Una donna a quindici anni* — she cannot have been much older — making us all wish that we could reconnect with our inner 17-year-old. As she evanesced out of earshot, the Frenchman warmed to his theme. 'I suppose you think that no one should take her to bed until she's 60?' 'I'd settle for a three-year delay,' said one of our number who announced himself as the Faun's father. 'But I doubt I'll get it. Her current boyfriend's a lecherous young dog if ever I saw one.'

The rest of us envied the youth. Someone told the story of Justice Oliver Wendell Holmes, *aetat* 90, chatting to a fellow judge of the same vintage: let us call him Smith. A girl law clerk sashayed past them. 'Ah, Smith,' said Holmes: 'to be 70 again.' The oenological argument continued. I am sure the British side was right about the Margaux, but the Frog would not countenance it. Like most of his male fellow-countrymen, he is convinced that only the French know how to appreciate wine, and women.

A few days later, more discussion of France, abetted by a lesser wine that was also perfect in its way. We were eating brisket, and agreeing that we ought to do so more often, especially in winter. It was cooked to perfection, and accompanied by a Savigny-lès-Beaune 2009, from the Domaine Jean-Jacques Girard. This would not pretend to be a great wine, but it is beautifully made and did just what it ought to do: suffuse and delight the palate with glorious pinot noir. We all agreed that this was a classic French repast: *comme chez grand-mère*. There was another Frenchman present who shook his head, not in derision, but in dismay. 'Alas,' he said, 'much of this bourgeois cuisine is now under threat. Young girls go out to work. They don't have time to spend hours in the kitchen, as their mothers did. The skills will be lost.

'As for restaurants, there are two problems. The 35-hour week has messed up restaurant economics. So has female emancipation. Those old places in the provinces: *le Patron mange ici*. So he did, and he didn't half *mange* well, while *sa femme, ses filles* and every other family female he could conscript *travaillent ici*. And they didn't half *travaille*. *Le Patron* would be offering his *copains* another Armagnac at gone three o'clock while the girls were finishing the dishes and starting on dinner. Now, the younger generation would not stand for it.'

We have to preserve French culinary culture. Civilisation demands no less. So I offered a *concorde* to the second Frenchman. We will acknowledge your supremacy in female husbandry, including the drinking age of that most coquettish of clarets, Château Margaux, as long as you will ensure that the French kitchen remains an emancipation-free zone.

# ~ Clubbable bottles ~

Gentlemen's clubs attract far more interest than they deserve, and an equally unmerited degree of mistrust. If they are not the establishment in secret conclave, they must surely be a potent means of networking — and they exclude women. As for the establishment charge: if only. The country would be better run. The networking allegation, popular with female journalists, is easy to dismiss. Chaps go to their clubs to get away from business, not to be reminded of it.

Two editorial types who are old friends have managed to organise a drop of luncheon at the Garrick, which is increasingly difficult these days. There is always someone with a clipboard wanting a two o'clock meeting to discuss photocopying requirements for the third quarter of 2013. After their meal, they are having a digestif in that snug under the stairs. Would it be wise for some youth to appear, offering his services as an assistant features editor? Network: he might find that it was tightening around his throat. Anyway, a pretty girl journalist has far better opportunities to make contacts than her male contemporaries do.

Clubs are not serious places. They are about fun, laughter and talk. On the average members' table, the conversation can switch in an instant from bawdry to books; from scandal to scholarship. There is also food and drink. Over the past 20 years, the quality of club cuisine has been transformed; most clubs now routinely produce good food. On occasions, especially during the game season, for 'good' read 'superb'. But alas, there has been one backsliding. In the eighties, many clubs bought first growths. There has been a melancholy, slow withdrawal, which is increasingly affecting the super-seconds as well. The same is true of Oxbridge colleges. It is sad to think that within a few years, the wine lists in the new gentlemen's clubs of Beijing and Shanghai will be better than anything in Pall Mall or St James's.

So, carpe diem. Club members and their guests can still benefit from the wisdom of wine committees in earlier days, before the balance of power moved in favour of the Far East. One of my clubs has always specialised in Calon-Ségur, a wine that has often been underrated because it is a proper old-fashioned Left-Banker with none of the jammy flamboyance which excites Robert Parker. It was a bottle of '88 Calon-Ségur which introduced the deputy editor of *The Spectator* to the pleasure of serious claret. We are now drinking the 1996. It is everything that mature claret ought to be.

Or rather, almost everything. About five years ago, waiting for a friend in Brooks's, I had a glance at their wine list. An '86 Lafite, at £125 a bottle: even then, that was a bargain. Today, *Decanter* quotes it at over £15,000 a case. I thought that through another club, I could dine in Brooks's on Fridays. So I decided to taunt and tempt a girl who had always taken a stern line on institutions which debarred her sex from membership. I had tried unavailingly to reason with her: 'A hundred years ago, you wouldn't even have had a vote. Don't make the Africans' mistake: grab everything at once and end up in chaos.'

Claret succeeded where reason failed. 'Would you like to drink some '86 Lafite?' Sharp indrawal of breath. 'In Brooks's.' Confused breathing noises. 'Remember: if you don't, it'll all be drunk by men.' Pause. 'All right.' I am not going to try to describe that wine, so please take the superlatives as read. There was only one little local difficulty. A couple of days later, I ran into the Secretary of Brooks's, who gave me a rueful look. Although his front desk had accepted my booking, we were both in error. That other club did not have dining rights on Fridays. Even if it had done, the Lafite was not available to reciprocals: members only, strictly rationed. I apologised and commiserated. But I have never felt more hypocritical.

## ~ Stars by any other name ~

*Eheu fugaces.* It is 1989 and I am off to Paris for the *Sunday Telegraph*, to cover the Sommet de l'Arche. Intended to commemorate the French Revolution's bicentenary, it was a characteristic Gallic blend of *grand projet*, grandiloquence and frippery. The late Frank Johnson makes a suggestion. I ought to talk to Serge July, the editor of *Libération*, who is very close to Mitterrand; and here is a number for someone who will have M. July's coordinates. Already halfway out of the door, not fully concentrating, I thought I was writing down July's number.

I phoned it on landing, and asked for Serge July. 'Do you mean Georges Joly?' Perhaps I did. Put through, I told him that I was a colleague of Frank Johnson's. 'Ah, Monsieur: mon vieil ami Johnson. Bienvenue à Paris. Qu'est-ce que vous faites pour diner ce soir? Je vous propose un petit restaurant du quartier.' Good old Frank, I thought, and I asked if I could come round that afternoon with a *cahier*: it might be an idea to work through a few complexities before we both got dined. Although there was a gracious 'bien sûr', M. Joly seemed surprised. On arrival, I knew that something was wrong. This was not the editorial office of a left-wing newspaper. I pressed on. Mitterrand had just been out-voted 11 to one at a European Council. What was going on? The alarmed expression on my interlocutor's face was rising towards panic. 'Pourquoi vous *me* demandez ça?' I said that our friend Johnson had told me that he was a very distinguished editor, able to unravel the intricacies of French foreign policy. 'C'est vrai, je suis redacteur, mais d'un journal de cuisine et de bons vins. Politique: je m'y intéresse peu et je n'y connais rien.' Poor M. Joly had mistaken me for a friend of Hugh Johnson, the wine writer. Before he could summon the men in white coats, I made my excuses and left, with a final placatory inquiry: where could one find three-rosette cooking at one-rosette prices? As if trying to appease the wolves pursuing the troika, he almost flung a couple of guide books at me. Alas, they did not answer my question.

The search for the three in one extends to wine. How can we replace the first growths — and indeed the seconds — now priced beyond all affordability? There is one partial solution. In France, there are strict regulations as to how much a given vineyard can bottle under its own name. Fortunately, the Frogs are not always as insouciant about rules as we Rosbifs claim. Good winemakers have a lot of defrocked wine. Inevitably, many of those bottles never travel far. Too many locals know their true value. So does the publisher of Everyman books, David Campbell.

At Everyman, David has a French assistant who says that her name is Dominatrix. During the shooting season, she does have to ensure that David will occasionally visit the office. Sultry, pouting and subtle, she has the soul of Edith Piaf in the body of Jeanne Moreau. When visitors become too bewitched, she mentions her boyfriend. He is in the Foreign Legion. He is two metres tall.

David himself is a sort of French foreign legion. He has not only visited the hauts lieux, he knows the 'B' roads. His love for France has been reciprocated, by the award of the Légion d'Honneur, and by contacts who enable him to acquire declassified wines. He helps to run From Vineyards Direct, an outstanding source of reasonably priced wine. At the moment, they are offering bottles that can only be sold as Pauillac, Margaux and St-Julien. They are defrocked Pichon-Longueville Baron, Palmer and Ducru-Beaucaillou. He also has a Sauternes, Haut Charmes, which is made by Yquem. At a fraction of the price of their siblings, these are all bargains. There is only one disappointment. Apropos defrocking, Dominatrix is not involved in From Vineyards Direct.

# ~ The single European goose ~

I have discovered a powerful argument in favour of ever-closer union with Europe and cannot think why the federasts have not used it. A girl I know who is a professional cook had been using Selfridges as a speakeasy. Although the shop had banned the sale of foie gras, a good butcher with a franchise on the premises would act as a bootlegger. If you asked him for French fillet, he would provide foie gras. Alas, the Selfridges food police found out and closed him down. We should all boycott the House of Selfridge until it comes to its senses.

So where was the EU? What is wrong with a common European foie gras policy? It should be illegal for Selfridges to refuse to sell the stuff. Equally, British laws which ban its production should be struck down. If it is lawful to make the stuff in Périgord, the same should apply in Potter's Bar. The late Bron Waugh considered going into the foie gras business on his Somerset acres, far enough from London to be beyond the reach of the law courts. According to his researches, the geese enjoyed their meals and would greet the 'gorgeuse' with a joyous waddle. There was one drawback. It would take an hour of female labour per diem to funnel enough grain down the goose's gullet. But such a repetitive task does not require a high-class workforce. The dimmest girl from the boggiest-standard comprehensive should be up to it. A British foie gras industry is overdue.

At the time of the millennium, I had an instructive foie gras experience. It was during a well-supplied house party in Bruges. The cleaning woman's boyfriend was thinking of going into the foie gras trade — imagine that in Potter's Bar — and had given the house a large bloc of pâté to advertise his wares. It was as good as the foie gras I had eaten at the Gavroche just before Christmas. We ate half at dinner, but the next morning there was none left for a pre-lunch *amuse-gueule*. Your correspondent fell under suspicion, as did a brace of Cecils. Public opinion took the view that the three of us had the necessary combination of amorality and gluttony to perpetrate such a crime. Then the culprit was revealed: a female American banker. Not that she had even eaten the pâté, which would have entitled her to the Flemish female all-time foie gras-scoffing trophy. No, she had thrown it away. There were two lessons from this. First, when precious foodstuffs are at stake, do not trust the girls to clear the dining table without supervision. Second, the errant female was not an equal-opportunity appointment. She was a plausible aspirant to senior banking. But people who maltreat super-prime foie gras are not fit to be left in charge of sub-prime mortgages. It should have been possible to extrapolate from that lost foie gras to the banking crisis.

Assuming that you succeed in acquiring foie gras and protecting it from American bankers, what should you drink with it? There are lots of serious pudding wines, including those from Germany, Alsace, Hungary and the New World, which all work. But if you are fortunate enough to be adjacent to a bottle of Yquem, there is nothing finer; that truly is pâté de foie gras to the sound of trumpets.

I know: the price is atrocious, and there are other Sauternes and Barsacs which can seem almost as good. 'Seem' is the word. The longer it is since one has tasted that Sun God of a wine, the more plausible its rivals will seem. Then, the first sip, and hierarchy is restored. But there is a further alternative: Ygrec, Yquem's drier cousin, which I first tasted over dinner with the late Ian Gilmour. I had some with foie gras over the New Year. It was a subtle and piquant experience and Ygrec is not so hideously expensive as its kinsman. That leads on to the obvious New Year resolution: eat as much foie gras as possible, accompanied, whenever possible, by Yquem or Ygrec.

'Need any more be said..........'